The Call of the Wild

Jack London

THE EMC MASTERPIECE SERIES

Access Editions

SERIES EDITOR

Robert D. Shepherd

EMC/Paradigm Publishing
St. Paul, Minnesota

Staff Credits:

For **EMC/Paradigm Publishing**, St. Paul, Minnesota

Laurie Skiba
Editor

Eileen Slater
Editorial Consultant

Shannon O'Donnell Taylor
Associate Editor

For **Penobscot School Publishing, Inc.**, Danvers, Massachusetts

Editorial

Robert D. Shepherd
President, Executive Editor

Christina Kolb
Managing Editor

Kim Leahy Beaudet
Editor

Sara Hyry
Editor

Marilyn Murphy Shepherd
Editor

Sharon Salinger
Copyeditor

Design and Production

Charles Q. Bent
Production Manager

Sara Day
Art Director

Tatiana Cicuto
Compositor

ISBN 0–8219–1615–7

Published by EMC/Paradigm Publishing
875 Montreal Way
St. Paul, Minnesota 55102

Printed in the United States of America.
10 9 8 7 6 5 4 3 2 xxx 02 01 00 99 98 97

Table of Contents

Jack London

Jack London

Jack London (1876-1916). London was born in San Francisco, California, to Flora Wellman Chaney. His father had deserted the family before he was born. When London was nine months old, his mother married John London, a widower with two daughters. Because of the family's severe poverty, Jack left school at the age of fourteen to work in a cannery, and he experienced the colorful life of the San Francisco waterfront. By the age of sixteen, London had been both an oyster pirate and a member of the San Francisco Bay Fish Patrol. In 1893, at the age of seventeen, London joined the crew of a sealing schooner called the *Sophia Sutherland* and traveled on an eight-month expedition as far away as Hawaii, Siberia, and Japan. Based on this experience, London wrote the essay "Story of a Typhoon off the Coast of Japan," which won a twenty-five-dollar first prize in a San Francisco newspaper contest. After his experience at sea, London worked as a coal heaver in the power plant of Oakland, California, shoveling coal for ten cents an hour. Then he joined "Kelly's Army," a group of unemployed men marching to Washington to protest poor economic conditions. After leaving Kelly's Army and serving time in prison for vagrancy, London toured the East Coast and then returned to the West Coast by train, traveling across Canada on a coal car. He earned passage on a ship going from Vancouver to California by stoking coal.

On his return to Oakland, London became determined to become a writer; he read voraciously and, at the age of nineteen, continued his education at Oakland High School. After one semester at the University of California, London joined countless others in the Klondike Gold Rush. He spent a winter on Split-Up Island, eight miles from the major community of the Klondike Region, Dawson City. Ill with scurvy, he returned to Oakland and began writing seriously, focusing on his Northland experiences. At the age of twenty-three, London made his literary breakthrough with the story "An Odyssey of the North," which was published by the *Atlantic Monthly* magazine in 1899. Another notable piece published during this time was "To the Man on the Trail," which appeared in the *Overland Monthly*. He also published about twenty other stories, essays, and poems.

London wrote over two hundred short stories in the next twenty years. During that time he also published twenty novels, more than four hundred nonfiction pieces, and three plays. Despite the extraordinary variety of subjects explored in his work, London's reputation as a writer was based largely on his works about the great North Country. These works included twenty-eight short stories, four novels, one play, and six nonfiction pieces. London's writings about the North Country are, by and large, examples of Naturalism, a literary movement of the late nineteenth and early twentieth centuries that saw actions and events as arising inevitably from forces in the environment. London's most famous novels set in the North are *The Call of the Wild* (1903) and *White Fang* (1906). His other novels include *The Sea-Wolf* (1904), *The Game* (1905), *Martin Eden* (1909), *John Barleycorn* (1913), and *Jerry of the Islands* (1917). His collections of short stories include *Love of Life* (1907), *Lost Face* (1910), and *On the Makaloa Mat* (1919).

Sickness plagued London throughout his thirties. At age thirty-one, he contracted tropical sicknesses in the Solomon Islands. At age thirty-seven, he underwent surgery for appendicitis and doctors discovered that his kidneys were diseased. The following year he hoped to report on the Mexican Revolution but was struck with dysentery. Two years later, at forty years of age, Jack London died of heart failure and a possible stroke. Despite this untimely death, London left a wide body of works. The works of Jack London greatly influenced many modern writers, including George Orwell and Ernest Hemingway. His works have been translated into over eighty languages and remain extremely popular today.

Biographical Time Line

1876   Jack Griffith is born in San Francisco, California. His father, William Henry Chaney, deserts the family, but his mother marries a man named John London when Jack is nine months old.

1878   The family moves to Oakland, California, where John runs a grocery store.

1881   The family moves to a farm in Alameda, and Jack starts grade school.

1890   London leaves school to work in a cannery. A few months later he purchases a boat and becomes an oyster pirate on San Francisco Bay.

1892   London serves for nearly a year as a deputy fish patrolman in the Fish Patrol of San Francisco Bay.

1893   London sails to Japan and Siberia on a seal-hunting voyage. Based on this experience, he writes a prize-winning essay called "Story of a Typhoon off the Coast of Japan," published in the *San Francisco Morning Call*.

1894   London works as a coal-heaver in the power plant of Oakland. He joins a group called "Kelly's Army," travels around the Midwest and the East Coast, and is arrested for vagrancy in Niagara.

1895   London decides to become a writer and returns to high school in Oakland.

1897   London joins the Gold Rush to the Klondike, where he spends two years. His search for gold is unsuccessful, but the setting inspires many of his most successful novels and stories.

1899   London gets his first literary break: He publishes a story, "An Odyssey of the North," in the *Atlantic Monthly* magazine.

1900   London publishes a collection of stories, *The Son of Wolf*. By this time he is a popular and well-paid writer.

1903   London publishes the novel *The Call of the Wild*, which confirms his status as a great American writer. He also publishes *The People of the Abyss*, a book influenced by the theory of Social Darwinism.

1904   London publishes the novel *The Sea-Wolf*.

1906   London publishes the novel *White Fang*.

1910   London settles near Glen Ellen, California. He publishes the novel *Revolution*.

1913   London's house burns down.

1916   London dies on November 22, at the age of forty.

Historical Time Line

Colorado is admitted to the Union; Lieutenant George Custer and white soldiers are defeated by the Sioux in the Battle of Little Big Horn.

1876

Rutherford B. Hayes becomes president.

1877

James Abram Garfield is elected president.

1880

President Garfield is assassinated. Chester Alan Arthur succeeds as president.

1881

Grover Cleveland is elected president; Alaska becomes a district governed by the laws of the state of Oregon.

1884

North Dakota, South Dakota, Montana, and Washington are admitted to the Union.

1889

The last major military battle between whites and Native Americans—the Battle of Wounded Knee—takes place in South Dakota.

1890

Grover Cleveland is elected to a second term as president.

1892

William McKinley is elected president. Gold is discovered in the Klondike region of Canada.

1896

People rush to stake claims in the Klondike. The United States annexes Hawaii.

1897

The Spanish-American War, a conflict between Spain and the United States, is fought in Cuba and the Philippines.

1898

President McKinley is assassinated. Theodore Roosevelt succeeds as president.

1901

Gold is discovered in the Fairbanks region of Alaska.

1902

President Roosevelt is reelected.

1904

William Taft is elected president.

1908

The National Association for the Advancement of Colored People (NAACP) is founded.

1910

Woodrow Wilson is elected president. The *Titanic* sinks.

1912

World War I begins.

1914

President Wilson is reelected.

1916

Historical Overview

The Klondike Gold Rush

The Call of the Wild is a novel inspired by Jack London's experiences during the Klondike Gold Rush in the Yukon Territory of northwest Canada. Like many other Klondike gold-seekers, London was attracted to the Yukon Territory because of its promise of wealth, and because the rugged area, known to many as the "Last Frontier," was an ideal place to test one's courage, adaptability, and endurance.

The Yukon Territory is bordered by the Arctic Ocean to the north, the Northwest Territory to the east, British Columbia to the south, and Alaska to the west. The Klondike River crosses the territory and enters the Yukon River at the major city of Dawson. In 1896, gold deposits were discovered in Rabbit (now Bonanza) Creek, which is a tributary, or branch, of the Klondike River. News of gold in the Klondike region of the Yukon Territory reached the United States in 1897, attracting thousands of prospectors. The term *prospector* comes from a Latin word meaning "to seek." Traveling to this wild, cold area and then surviving in it was not easy. The region was nearly uninhabited at the time the first deposits of gold were found. Many people never even made it to the areas that were richest in gold. After the most easily accessible deposits were exhausted, people tried to travel further into the Yukon interior. Out of nearly two hundred and fifty thousand prospectors attempting this journey, only about fifty thousand actually completed it. Enough prospectors did make it to cause the area to experience a sharp rise in population. After just four years of the gold rush, thirty thousand people had arrived to mine gold. Prospectors faced many hardships in the region, including near-famine conditions during winter months.

Despite hardships, $100 million in gold was mined in the Yukon Territory within ten years of the start of the Gold Rush. The highest annual output in gold was $22 million in 1900. From that point on, there was a steady decline in production. By 1910, many people had left the area, having moved on to Alaska and other northern regions. The Yukon Territory still produces small amounts of gold and silver, as well as other minerals, such as lead. The great gold rushes of the nineteenth century were one expression of the frontier spirit—the desire to explore and to settle open territory—that shaped North American culture during that time. When this period ended, mining was largely taken over by corporations and governments.

London was attracted to the Yukon Territory in part because of his personal philosophy, which was based on the theory of Social Darwinism. He believed the idea that human societies are or should be managed according to the principle of "survival of the fittest," and this idea seemed to be lived out fully in the wild and harsh Yukon Territory, where laws and law enforcement were virtually nonexistent. In *The Call of the Wild*, London's Social Darwinism is combined with Naturalism, a literary movement of the late nineteenth and early twentieth centuries that saw actions and events as resulting inevitably from biological or natural forces or from forces in the environment. In works of Naturalism, actions and events are often beyond the comprehension and control of the characters subjected to them. London believed that when civilizing influences and conditions are absent, peoples' essentially uncivilized and wild natures come out. The influence of Social Darwinism; the frontier virtues of courage, individuality, endurance, and intelligence; and the experience of surviving a winter eight miles out of Dawson in the Yukon Territory are all reflected in *The Call of the Wild*.

List of Characters

Dogs

Buck. Buck, part Saint Bernard and part Scottish shepherd, is the main character of the novel. During the course of this novel, Buck changes from a pampered, civilized dog from the south to an animal who can survive in the rugged north. Buck's experiences illustrate Jack London's belief in the principle of "survival of the fittest."

Curly. Curly is Buck's friend, whom he meets on the boat trip to the north. She is good natured and has trouble adapting.

Spitz. This dog becomes Buck's enemy. He has a violent fight with Buck that is significant because it shows that Buck is trying to adapt and survive in his new environment.

Toots and Ysabel. These are two small dogs who live on Judge Miller's estate with Buck—a Japanese pug and a Mexican hairless.

Dave, Joe, Billee, Dolly, Pike, Sol-leks, and Dub. These dogs are on Perrault and Francois's sled team with Buck.

Skeet and Nig. These are two of John Thornton's dogs.

People

Judge Miller. Judge Miller is Buck's first owner. The judge pampers Buck and treats him as a member of his family. Buck's father had been his constant companion.

Manuel. Manuel is a gardener's helper on Judge Miller's estate.

Man in the Red Sweater. This man is the first person to teach Buck a "primitive law"—that Buck cannot win a fight against a man wielding a weapon. This lesson stays with Buck throughout the book.

Perrault and François. These two Frenchmen are Buck's first owners in the North. They work for the Canadian government, carrying mail to different outposts.

The Scot. This man buys Buck from Perrault and Francois. He delivers mail and works his dogs hard.

Charles. This man is Buck's third master in the north. He is incompetent as a sled driver and continually puts himself and the dogs at risk because he does not understand the north.

Mercedes. She is Charles's wife. She, also, does not understand how to survive in the dangerous north. She thinks of their journey as a type of camping trip.

Hal. He is Mercedes's brother. He carries weapons and mistreats Buck.

John Thornton. John Thornton saves Buck's life, and, in turn, Buck feels a responsibility to protect him at all times.

Hans and Pete. These men are John Thornton's partners. They travel with him to pan for gold in the lost mine.

Matthewson. This man bets John Thornton that Buck cannot pull a sled holding a thousand pounds.

Jim O'Brien. This man is a friend of John Thornton's. He offers to lend Thornton money to make the bet with Matthewson.

The Yeehats. The Yeehat Indians come to think of Buck as the Evil Spirit.

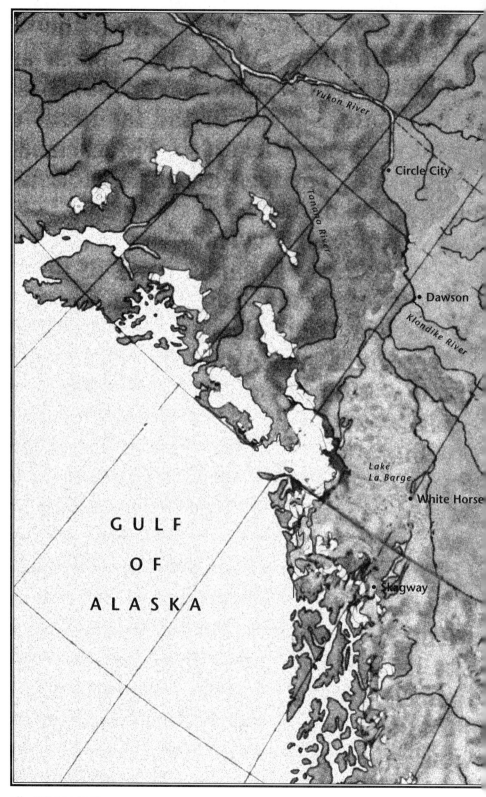

Yukon River

Circle City

Tanana River

Dawson

Klondike River

Lake
La Barge

White Horse

GULF

OF

ALASKA

Skagway

ARCTIC CIRCLE

A dog becomes the leader of a team of sled dogs by inspiring fear and respect in the others. Dogfights break out when the dominance of the leader is contested.

People use the Siberian husky as a sled dog in the Arctic regions because of its ability to endure extremely cold temperatures. This rugged animal has been known to weigh as much as 130 pounds.

Prospectors carried only the essentials on their backs—a stock of preserved food, warm blankets, and a change of clothes. They wore a hat and a good pair of boots to protect head and feet from the cold.

A prospector would fill his washpan with mud, immerse it in a river, and shake it. Gold dust and nuggets, being heavier, would remain at the bottom of the pan, while earth drained off.

A team of six to eight dogs can easily pull a person and a sled full of baggage.

CHAPTER I

Into the Primitive

"Old longings nomadic leap,
Chafing at custom's chain;
Again from its brumal[1] sleep
Wakens the ferine[2] strain."

Buck did not read the newspapers, or he would have known that trouble was brewing, not alone for himself, but for every tidewater dog, strong of muscle and with warm, long hair, from Puget Sound to San Diego. Because men, groping in the Arctic darkness, had found a yellow metal,[3] and because steamship and transportation companies were booming the find, thousands of men were rushing into the Northland. These men wanted dogs, and the dogs they wanted were heavy dogs, with strong muscles by which to toil, and furry coats to protect them from the frost.

◀ Who wants dogs? Why do they want dogs?

Buck lived at a big house in the sun-kissed Santa Clara Valley. Judge Miller's place, it was called. It stood back from the road, half hidden among the trees, through which glimpses could be caught of the wide cool veranda that ran around its four sides. The house was approached by graveled driveways which wound about through wide-spreading lawns and under the interlacing boughs of tall poplars. At the rear, things were on even a more spacious scale than at the front. There were great stables, where a

---

1. **brumal.** Wintry
2. **ferine.** Feral; untamed or wild
3. **yellow metal.** Gold

Words For Everyday Use	no • mad • ic (nō mad´ ik) *adj.*, wandering, moving about constantly
	ve • ran • da (və ran´də) *n.*, open porch

dozen grooms and boys held forth, rows of vine-clad servants' cottages, an endless and orderly array of outhouses, long grape arbors, green pastures, orchards, and berry patches. Then there was the pumping plant for the artesian well,[4] and the big cement tank where Judge Miller's boys took their morning plunge and kept cool in the hot afternoon.

And over this great <u>demesne</u> Buck ruled. Here he was born, and here he had lived the four years of his life. It was true, there were other dogs. There could not but be other dogs on so vast a place, but they did not count. They came and went, resided in the populous kennels, or lived <u>obscurely</u> in the <u>recesses</u> of the house after the fashion of Toots, the Japanese pug, or Ysabel, the Mexican hairless, strange creatures that rarely put nose out of doors or set foot to ground. On the other hand, there were the fox terriers, a score of them at least, who yelped fearful promises at Toots and Ysabel looking out of the windows at them and protected by a legion of housemaids armed with brooms and mops.

But Buck was neither house-dog nor kennel-dog. The whole realm was his. He plunged into the swimming tank or went hunting with the Judge's sons; he escorted Mollie and Alice, the Judge's daughters, on long twilight or early morning rambles; on wintry nights he lay at the Judge's feet before the roaring library fire; he carried the Judge's grandsons on his back, or rolled them in the grass, and guarded their footsteps through wild adventures down to the fountain in the stable yard, and even beyond, where the <u>paddocks</u> were, and the berry patches. Among

▶ *What details show Buck's high status at the Judge's place?*

---

4. **artesian well.** Well drilled deep enough to reach water that is draining from higher ground, so that pressure will force a flow upward

Words For Everyday Use

de • mesne (di mān´) *n.*, region; domain
ob • scure • ly (əb skyo͞or´lē) *adv.*, unnoticed
re • cess (rē´ses) *n.*, secluded place
pad • dock (pad´ək) *n.*, enclosed field

the terriers he stalked <u>imperiously</u>, and Toots and Ysabel he utterly ignored, for he was king—king over all creeping, crawling, flying things of Judge Miller's place, humans included.

His father, Elmo, a huge St. Bernard, had been the Judge's inseparable companion, and Buck bid fair to follow[5] in the way of his father. He was not so large—he weighed only one hundred and forty pounds—for his mother, Shep, had been a Scotch shepherd dog. Nevertheless, one hundred and forty pounds, to which was added the dignity that comes of good living and universal respect, enabled him to carry himself in right royal fashion. During the four years since his puppyhood he had lived the life of a <u>sated</u> aristocrat; he had a fine pride in himself, was even a trifle egotistical, as country gentlemen sometimes become because of their <u>insular</u> situation. But he had saved himself by not becoming a mere pampered house-dog. Hunting and kindred outdoor delights had kept down the fat and hardened his muscles; and to him, as to the cold-tubbing races, the love of water had been a tonic and a health preserver.

◀ *What words and details are used to portray Buck's character?*

And this was the manner of dog Buck was in the fall of 1897, when the Klondike[6] strike dragged men from all the world into the frozen North. But Buck did not read the newspapers, and he did not know that Manuel, one of the gardener's helpers, was an undesirable acquaintance. Manuel had one <u>besetting</u> sin. He loved to play Chinese lottery. Also, in his gambling, he had one besetting weakness—faith in a system; and this made his damnation certain.

---

5. **bid fair to follow.** Seemed likely to follow
6. **Klondike.** Gold was found in 1896 in the Klondike, a river in West Yukon Territory, Canada.

| Words For Everyday Use | im • per • i • ous • ly (im pir´ē es lē) *adv.*, with an overbearing or imperial manner
sat • ed (sāt´əd) *adj.*, satisfied
in • su • lar (in´sə lər) *adj.*, detached; isolated | be • set • ting (bē set´ŋ) *part.*, constantly harassing |

For to play a system requires money, while the wages of a gardener's helper do not lap over the needs of a wife and numerous progeny.

The Judge was at a meeting of the Raisin Growers' Association, and the boys were busy organizing an athletic club, on the memorable night of Manuel's treachery. No one saw him and Buck go off through the orchard on what Buck imagined was merely a stroll. And with the exception of a solitary man, no one saw them arrive at the little flag station known as College Park. This man talked with Manuel, and money chinked between them.

► What does
Manuel do to Buck?

"You might wrap up the goods before you deliver 'm," the stranger said gruffly, and Manuel doubled a piece of stout rope around Buck's neck under the collar.

"Twist it, an' you'll choke 'm plentee," said Manuel, and the stranger grunted a ready affirmative.

Buck had accepted the rope with quiet dignity. To be sure, it was an unwonted performance: but he had learned to trust in men he knew, and to give them credit for a wisdom that outreached his own. But when the ends of the rope were placed in the stranger's hands, he growled menacingly. He had merely intimated his displeasure, in his pride believing that to intimate was to command. But to his surprise the rope tightened around his neck, shutting off his breath. In quick rage he sprang at the man, who met him halfway, grappled him close by the throat, and with a deft twist threw him over on his back. Then the rope tightened mercilessly, while Buck struggled in a fury, his tongue lolling out of his mouth and his great chest panting futilely. Never in all his life had he been so vilely treated, and never in all his life had he been so angry. But his strength

► What are Buck's
first reactions to
captivity?

Words
For
Everyday
Use

prog • e • ny (präj´ə nē) n., descendant; offspring
un • won • ted (un wän´tid) adj., uncommon
in • ti • mate (in´tə māt´) vt., hint, imply
fu • tile • ly (fyoo´til´lē) adv., ineffectively

ebbed, his eyes glazed, and he knew nothing when the train was flagged and the two men threw him into the baggage car.

The next he knew, he was dimly aware that his tongue was hurting and that he was being jolted along in some kind of a <u>conveyance</u>. The hoarse shriek of a locomotive whistling a crossing told him where he was. He had traveled too often with the Judge not to know the sensation of riding in a baggage car. He opened his eyes, and into them came the unbridled anger of a kidnapped king. The man sprang for his throat, but Buck was too quick for him. His jaws closed on the hand, nor did they relax till his senses were choked out of him once more.

◄ *Where is Buck? How does he know where he is?*

"Yep, has fits," the man said, hiding his mangled hand from the baggageman, who had been attracted by the sounds of struggle. "I'm takin' 'm up for the boss to 'Frisco. A crack dog-doctor there thinks that he can cure 'm."

Concerning that night's ride, the man spoke most eloquently for himself, in a little shed back of a saloon on the San Francisco waterfront.

"All I get is fifty for it," he grumbled; "an' I wouldn't do it over for a thousand, cold cash."

His hand was wrapped in a bloody handkerchief, and the right trouser leg was ripped from knee to ankle.

"How much did the other mug get?" the saloon-keeper demanded.

"A hundred," was the reply. "Wouldn't take a sou[7] less, so help me."

"That makes a hundred and fifty," the saloon-keeper calculated; "and he's worth it, or I'm a squarehead."

---

7. **sou.** Any of several antique French coins of very small denomination

Words For Everyday Use

con • vey • ance (kən vāʹəns) *n.,* carrying device

The kidnapper undid the bloody wrappings and looked at his <u>lacerated</u> hand. "If I don't get the hydrophoby—"[8]

"It'll be because you was born to hang," laughed the saloonkeeper. "Here, lend me a hand before you pull your freight," he added.

Dazed, suffering intolerable pain from throat and tongue, with the life half throttled out of him, Buck attempted to face his <u>tormentors</u>. But he was thrown down and choked repeatedly, till they succeeded in filing the heavy brass collar from off his neck. Then the rope was removed, and he was flung into a cage-like crate.

There he lay for the remainder of the weary night, nursing his wrath and wounded pride. He could not understand what it all meant. What did they want with him, these strange men? Why were they keeping him pent up in this narrow crate? He did not know why, but he felt oppressed by the vague sense of impending calamity. Several times during the night he sprang to his feet when the shed door rattled open, expecting to see the Judge, or the boys at least. But each time it was the bulging face of the saloonkeeper that peered in at him by the sickly light of a tallow candle. And each time the joyful bark that trembled in Buck's throat was twisted into a savage growl.

But the saloonkeeper let him alone, and in the morning four men entered and picked up the crate. More tormentors, Buck decided, for they were evil-looking creatures, ragged and unkempt; and he stormed and raged at them through the bars. They only laughed and poked sticks at him, which he

► *What hope does Buck still have? How does he feel when that hope is disappointed?*

---

8. **hydrophoby.** Hydrophobia, or rabies

| Words For Everyday Use | **lac • er • at • ed** (las´ər āt´ed) *part.,* cut; wounded |
| | **tor • men • tor** (tôr ment´ər) *n.,* one who causes great pain or suffering |

promptly assailed with his teeth till he realized that that was what they wanted. Whereupon he lay down <u>sullenly</u> and allowed the crate to be lifted into a wagon. Then he, and the crate in which he was imprisoned, began a passage through many hands. Clerks in the express office took charge of him; he was carted about in another wagon; a truck carried him, with an assortment of boxes and parcels, upon a ferry steamer; he was trucked off the steamer into a great railway depot, and finally he was deposited in an express car.

For two days and nights this express car was dragged along at the tail of shrieking locomotives; and for two days and nights Buck neither ate nor drank. In his anger he had met the first advances of the express messengers with growls, and they had retaliated by teasing him. When he flung himself against the bars, quivering and frothing, they laughed at him and taunted him. They growled and barked like detestable dogs, mewed, and flapped their arms and crowed. It was all very silly, he knew, but therefore the more outrage to his dignity, and his anger <u>waxed</u> and waxed. He did not mind the hunger so much, but the lack of water caused him severe suffering and fanned his wrath to fever-pitch. For that matter, high-strung and finely sensitive, the ill treatment had flung him into a fever, which was fed by the inflammation of his parched and swollen throat and tongue.

◀ *What behavior of the express messengers bothered Buck? Why did these actions anger him?*

He was glad for one thing: the rope was off his neck. That had given them an unfair advantage; but now that it was off, he would show them. They would never get another rope around his neck. Upon that he was <u>resolved</u>. For two days and nights he neither ate nor drank, and during those two days

Words For Everyday Use	**sul • len • ly** (sul´ən lē) *adv.*, showing resentment; gloomily **wax** (waks) *vi.*, increase in strength; grow larger **re • solved** (ri zälvd´) *adj.*, firm and fixed in purpose; determined

and nights of torment, he accumulated a fund of wrath that boded ill for whoever first fell foul of him. His eyes turned bloodshot, and he was meta-morphosed into a raging fiend. So changed was he that the Judge himself would not have recognized him; and the express messengers breathed with relief when they bundled him off the train at Seattle.

Four men gingerly carried the crate from the wagon into a small, high-walled back yard. A stout man, with a red sweater that sagged generously at the neck, came out and signed the book for the driver. That was the man, Buck divined, the next tormentor, and he hurled himself savagely against the bars. The man smiled grimly, and brought a hatchet and a club.

"You ain't going to take him out now?" the driver asked.

"Sure," the man replied, driving the hatchet into the crate for a pry.

There was an instantaneous scattering of the four men who had carried it in, and from safe perches on top of the wall they prepared to watch the performance.

Buck rushed at the splintering wood, sinking his teeth into it, surging and wrestling with it. Wherever the hatchet fell on the outside, he was there on the inside, snarling and growling, as furiously anxious to get out as the man in the red sweater was calmly intent on getting him out.

"Now, you red-eyed devil," he said, when he had made an opening sufficient for the passage of Buck's body. At the same time he dropped the hatchet and shifted the club to his right hand.

And Buck was truly a red-eyed devil, as he drew himself together for the spring, hair bristling, mouth foaming, a mad glitter in his bloodshot eyes. Straight

► How has Buck changed since he was taken from the Judge's place?

Words For Everyday Use

met • a • mor • phose (met´ə mor´fōz´) vt., change; transform
gin • ger • ly (jin´jər´lē) adv., cautiously
di • vine (də vīn´) vt., find out by intuition

at the man he launched his one hundred and forty pounds of fury, <u>surcharged</u> with the pent passion of two days and nights. In midair, just as his jaws were about to close on the man, he received a shock that checked his body and brought his teeth together with an agonizing clip. He whirled over, fetching the ground on his back and side. He had never been struck by a club in his life and did not understand. With a snarl that was part bark and more scream he was again on his feet and launched into the air. And again the shock came and he was brought crushingly to the ground. This time he was aware that it was the club, but his madness knew no caution. A dozen times he charged, and as often the club broke the charge and smashed him down.

After a particularly fierce blow he crawled to his feet, too dazed to rush. He staggered limply about, the blood flowing from nose and mouth and ears, his beautiful coat sprayed and flecked with bloody <u>slaver</u>. Then the man advanced and deliberately dealt him a frightful blow on the nose. All the pain he had endured was as nothing compared with the exquisite agony of this. With a roar that was almost lionlike in its ferocity, he again hurled himself at the man. But the man, shifting the club from right to left, coolly caught him by the under jaw, at the same time wrenching downward and backward. Buck described a complete circle in the air, and half of another, then crashed to the ground on his head and chest.

For the last time he rushed. The man struck the shrewd blow he had purposely withheld for so long, and Buck crumpled up and went down, knocked utterly senseless.

"He's no slouch at dog-breakin', that's wot I say," one of the men on the wall cried enthusiastically.

◀ What is the man trying to teach Buck?

"Druther[9] break cayuses[10] any day, and twice on Sundays," was the reply of the driver, as he climbed on the wagon and started the horses.

Buck's senses came back to him, but not his strength. He lay where he had fallen, and from there he watched the man in the red sweater.

"'Answers to the name of Buck,'" the man <u>soliloquized</u>, quoting from the saloonkeeper's letter which had announced the <u>consignment</u> of the crate and contents. "Well, Buck, my boy," he went on in a <u>genial</u> voice, "we've had our little ruction,[11] and the best thing we can do is to let it go at that. You've learned your place, and I know mine. Be a good dog and all 'll go well and the goose hang high. Be a bad dog, and I'll whale the stuffin' outa you. Understand?"

As he spoke he fearlessly patted the head he had so mercilessly pounded, and though Buck's hair involuntarily bristled at touch of the hand, he endured it without protest. When the man brought him water he drank eagerly, and later bolted a generous meal of raw meat, chunk by chunk, from the man's hand.

He was beaten (he knew that); but he was not broken. He saw, once for all, that he stood no chance against a man with a club. He had learned the lesson, and in all his afterlife he never forgot it. That was a revelation. It was his introduction to the reign of primitive law, and he met the introduction halfway. The facts of life took on a fiercer aspect; and while he faced that aspect <u>uncowed</u>, he faced it with all the <u>latent</u> cunning of his nature aroused. As the days went by, other dogs came, in crates and at the ends of ropes, some docilely, and some raging and roaring as he had

▶ *What lesson has Buck learned? How is this lesson significant?*

---

9. **Druther.** I'd rather
10. **cayuses.** Small western horses used by cowboys
11. **ruction.** Noisy disturbance or quarrel

so • lil • o • quize (sə lil´ə kwīz´) *vi.*, talk to oneself
con • sign • ment (kən sīn´mənt) *n.*, shipment
ge • ni • al (jēn´yəl) *adj.*, amiable; cheerful
un • cowed (un koud´) *part.*, unafraid; unintimidated
la • tent (lāt´nt) *adj.*, hidden

come; and, one and all, he watched them pass under the dominion of the man in the red sweater. Again and again, as he looked at each brutal performance, the lesson was driven home to Buck: a man with a club was a lawgiver, a master to be obeyed, though not necessarily <u>conciliated</u>. Of this last Buck was never guilty, though he did see beaten dogs that fawned upon the man, and wagged their tails, and licked his hand. Also he saw one dog, that would neither conciliate nor obey, finally killed in the struggle for mastery.

Now and again men came, strangers, who talked excitedly, wheedlingly, and in all kinds of fashions to the man in the red sweater. And at such times that money passed between them the strangers took one or more of the dogs away with them. Buck wondered where they went, for they never came back; but the fear of the future was strong upon him, and he was glad each time when he was not selected.

Yet his time came, in the end, in the form of a little weazened[12] man who spat broken English and many strange and <u>uncouth</u> exclamations which Buck could not understand.

"Sacredam!" he cried, when his eyes lit upon Buck. "Dat one dam bully dog! Eh? How moch?"

◄ Why does the man curse?

"Three hundred, and a present at that," was the prompt reply of the man in the red sweater. "And seein' it's government money, you ain't got no kick coming, eh, Perrault?"

Perrault grinned. Considering that the price of dogs had been boomed skyward by the unwonted demand, it was not an unfair sum for so fine an animal. The Canadian Government would be no loser, nor would its dispatches travel the slower. Perrault

---

12. **weazened.** Wizened (dried and shrunken, as from aging)

Words For Everyday Use

con • cil • i • ate (kən sil´ē āt´) vt., win over

un • couth (un kōōth´) adj., uncultured; crude; strange

knew dogs, and when he looked at Buck he knew that he was one in a thousand—"One in ten t'ousand," he commented mentally.

Buck saw money pass between them, and was not surprised when Curly, a good-natured Newfoundland, and he were led away by the little weazened man. That was the last he saw of the man in the red sweater, and as Curly and he looked at receding Seattle from the deck of the *Narwhal,* it was the last he saw of the warm Southland. Curly and he were taken below by Perrault and turned over to a black-faced giant called François. Perrault was a French-Canadian, and swarthy; François was a French-Canadian, and twice as swarthy. They were a new kind of men to Buck (of which he was destined to see many more), and while he developed no affection for them, he nonetheless grew honestly to respect them. He speedily learned that Perrault and François were fair men, calm and <u>impartial</u> in administering justice, and too wise in the way of dogs to be fooled by dogs.

In the 'tween-decks of the *Narwhal,* Buck and Curly joined two other dogs. One of them was a big, snow-white fellow from Spitzbergen who had been brought away by a whaling captain, and who had later accompanied a Geological Survey into the Barrens.[13] He was friendly, in a treacherous sort of way, smiling into one's face the while he meditated some underhand trick, as, for instance, when he stole from Buck's food at the first meal. As Buck sprang to punish him, the lash of François's whip sang through the air, reaching the culprit first; and nothing remained to Buck but to recover the bone.

---

13. **Barrens.** Extremely remote and sparsely populated region of the Northwest Territory, north and west of Hudson Bay, Canada

Words For Everyday Use	**im • par • tial** (im pär´shəl) *adj.,* without prejudice or bias

That was fair of François, he decided, and the man began his rise in Buck's estimation.

The other dog made no advances, nor received any; also, he did not attempt to steal from the newcomers. He was a gloomy, <u>morose</u> fellow, and he showed Curly plainly that all he desired was to be left alone, and further, that there would be trouble if he were not left alone. "Dave" he was called, and he ate and slept, or yawned between times, and took interest in nothing, not even when the *Narwhal* crossed Queen Charlotte Sound[14] and rolled and pitched and bucked like a thing possessed. When Buck and Curly grew excited, half wild with fear, he raised his head as though annoyed, favored them with an <u>incurious</u> glance, yawned, and went to sleep again.

Day and night the ship throbbed to the tireless pulse of the propeller, and though one day was very like another, it was apparent to Buck that the weather was steadily growing colder. At last, one morning, the propeller was quiet, and the *Narwhal* was <u>pervaded</u> with an atmosphere of excitement. He felt it, as did the other dogs, and knew that a change was at hand. François leashed them and brought them on deck. At the first step upon the cold surface, Buck's feet sank into a white mushy something very like mud. He sprang back with a snort. More of this white stuff was falling through the air. He shook himself, but more of it fell upon him. He sniffed it curiously, then licked some up on his tongue. It bit like fire, and the next instant was gone. This puzzled him. He tried it again, with the same result. The onlookers laughed uproariously, and he felt ashamed, he knew not why, for it was his first snow.

---

14. **Queen Charlotte Sound.** Body of water off the west coast of British Columbia, Canada

glossary

Words For Everyday Use	mo • rose (mə rōs´) *adj.*, ill-tempered; sullen
	in • cu • ri • ous (in kyo͞or´ē əs) *adj.*, uninterested
	per • vade (pər vād´) *vt.*, fill

Responding to the Selection

Imagine that you are the dog Buck in this novel. Suddenly, your world changes drastically. Imagine that you can communicate with the Judge back home. Tell him what has happened to you, expressing your feelings about some of the people you've met, such as the man in the red sweater.

Reviewing the Selection

Recalling and Interpreting

1. **R:** What kind of dog is Buck? What are some typical events in his life on the Judge's farm?

2. **I:** How would you characterize the kind of life that Buck enjoys on the Judge's farm?

3. **R:** What act of treachery does Manuel commit?

4. **I:** What causes a demand for strong-muscled, thick-coated dogs?

5. **R:** What is Buck's "introduction to the reign of primitive law"?

6. **I:** What causes Buck to sense that "the fear of the future was strong upon him"?

7. **R:** Who buys Buck from the man in the red sweater?

8. **I:** What does François do that begins "his rise in Buck's estimation"?

Synthesizing

9. What sort of relationship between humans and dogs exists on the Judge's farm? How does that differ from the relationship between the man in the red sweater and the dogs that cross his path?

10. In what kind of life is Buck learning his first lessons? What are those lessons?

Understanding Literature

1. Foreshadowing. Foreshadowing is the act of presenting materials that hint at events to occur later in a story. What events in this chapter foreshadow the kidnapping of Buck?

2. Conflict/Plot/Inciting Incident. A **conflict** is a struggle between two forces in a literary work. A **plot** is a series of events related to a central conflict in a literary work. A typical plot involves the following elements: introduction, inciting incident, rising action, climax, turning point, falling action, resolution, and dénouement. The **inciting incident** is the event that introduces the central conflict. What is the inciting incident that occurs in this opening chapter? What conflicts are introduced? Against what forces does Buck struggle?

CHAPTER II

The Law of Club and Fang

▶ How does life on the Dyea beach compare to life at the Judge's place?

Buck's first day on the Dyea beach was like a nightmare. Every hour was filled with shock and surprise. He had been suddenly jerked from the heart of civilization and flung into the heart of things <u>primordial</u>. No lazy, sun-kissed life was this, with nothing to do but loaf and be bored. Here was neither peace, nor rest, nor a moment's safety. All was confusion and action, and every moment life and limb were in peril. There was imperative need to be constantly alert; for these dogs and men were not town dogs and men. They were savages, all of them, who knew no law but the law of club and fang.

He had never seen dogs fight as these wolfish creatures fought, and his first experience taught him an unforgettable lesson. It is true, it was a <u>vicarious</u> experience, else he would not have lived to profit by it. Curly was the victim. They were camped near the log store, where she, in her friendly way, made advances to a husky dog the size of a full-grown wolf, though not half so large as she. There was no warning, only a leap in like a flash, a metallic clip of teeth, a leap out equally swift, and Curly's face was ripped open from eye to jaw.

▶ What happens to Curly? How do the other dogs react? How does Buck react?

It was the wolf manner of fighting, to strike and leap away; but there was more to it than this. Thirty or forty huskies ran to the spot and surrounded the combatants in an intent and silent circle. Buck did not comprehend that silent intentness, nor the eager way with which they were licking their chops.

Words For Everyday Use	pri • mor • dial (prī môr′dē əl) *adj.,* existing from the beginning of time; primitive
	vi • car • i • ous (vī ker′ē əs) *adj.,* experienced by imagined participation in another's experience

Curly rushed her <u>antagonist</u>, who struck again and leaped aside. He met her next rush with his chest, in a peculiar fashion that tumbled her off her feet. She never regained them. This was what the onlooking huskies had waited for. They closed in upon her, snarling and yelping, and she was buried, screaming with agony, beneath the bristling mass of bodies.

So sudden was it, and so unexpected, that Buck was taken aback. He saw Spitz run out his scarlet tongue in a way he had of laughing; and he saw François, swinging an axe, spring into the mess of dogs. Three men with clubs were helping him to scatter them. It did not take long. Two minutes from the time Curly went down, the last of her assailants were clubbed off. But she lay there limp and lifeless in the bloody, trampled snow, almost literally torn to pieces, the swart fellow standing over her and cursing horribly. The scene often came back to Buck to trouble him in his sleep. So that was the way. No fair play. Once down, that was the end of you. Well, he would see to it that he never went down. Spitz ran out his tongue and laughed again, and from that moment Buck hated him with a bitter and deathless hatred.

Before he had recovered from the shock caused by the tragic passing of Curly, he received another shock. François fastened upon him an arrangement of straps and buckles. It was a harness, such as he had seen the grooms put on the horses at home. And as he had seen horses work, so he was set to work, hauling François on a sled to the forest that fringed the valley, and returning with a load of firewood. Though his dignity was sorely hurt by thus being made a draft animal, he was too wise to rebel. He buckled down with a will and did his best, though it was all new and strange. François was stern,

◀ *What is Buck made to do? How does he feel about this? How does he respond?*

Words For Everyday Use

an • tag • o • nist (an tag´ə nist) *n.*, opponent; enemy

demanding instant obedience, and by virtue of his whip receiving instant obedience; while Dave, who was an experienced wheeler,[1] nipped Buck's hindquarters whenever he was in error. Spitz was the leader, likewise experienced, and while he could not always get at Buck, he growled sharp <u>reproof</u> now and again, or cunningly threw his weight in the traces to jerk Buck into the way he should go. Buck learned easily, and under the combined tuition of his two mates and François made remarkable progress. Ere they returned to camp he knew enough to stop at "ho," to go ahead at "mush," to swing wide on the bends, and to keep clear of the wheeler when the loaded sled shot downhill at their heels.

"T'ree vair' good dogs," François told Perrault. "Dat Buck, heem pool lak hell. I tich heem queek as anyt'ing."

By afternoon, Perrault, who was in a hurry to be on the trail with his dispatches, returned with two more dogs. "Billee" and "Joe" he called them, two brothers, and true huskies both. Sons of the one mother though they were, they were as different as day and night. Billee's one fault was his excessive good nature, while Joe was the very opposite, sour and <u>introspective</u>, with a perpetual snarl and a <u>malignant</u> eye. Buck received them in comradely fashion, Dave ignored them, while Spitz proceeded to thrash first one and then the other. Billee wagged his tail appeasingly, turned to run when he saw that appeasement was of no avail, and cried (still appeasingly) when Spitz's sharp teeth scored his flank. But no matter how Spitz circled, Joe whirled around on his heels to face him, mane

---

1. **wheeler.** One who urges on animals that pull a cart or sled

Words For Everyday Use	**re • proof** (ri prō̅of´) *n.*, rebuke; censure; chastisement
	in • tro • spec • tive (in´trō spek´tiv) *adj.*, looking within one's own mind
	ma • lig • nant (mə lig´nənt) *adj.*, wishing evil; dangerous

bristling, ears laid back, lips writhing and snarling, jaws clipping together as fast as he could snap, and eyes diabolically gleaming—the incarnation of belligerent fear. So terrible was his appearance that Spitz was forced to forego disciplining him, but to cover his own discomfiture he turned upon the inoffensive and wailing Billee and drove him to the confines of the camp.

By evening Perrault secured another dog, an old husky, long and lean and gaunt, with a battle-scarred face and a single eye, which flashed a warning of prowess that commanded respect. He was called Sol-leks, which means the Angry One. Like Dave, he asked nothing, gave nothing, expected nothing; and when he marched slowly and deliberately into their midst, even Spitz left him alone. He had one peculiarity which Buck was unlucky enough to discover. He did not like to be approached on his blind side. Of this offense Buck was unwittingly guilty, and the first knowledge he had of his indiscretion was when Sol-leks whirled upon him and slashed his shoulder to the bone for three inches up and down. Forever after Buck avoided his blind side, and to the last of their comradeship had no more trouble. His only apparent ambition, like Dave's, was to be left alone; though, as Buck was afterward to learn, each of them possessed one other and even more vital ambition.

That night Buck faced the great problem of sleeping. The tent, illumined by a candle, glowed warmly in the midst of the white plain; and when he, as a matter of course, entered it, both Perrault and François bombarded him with curses and cooking utensils, till he recovered from his consternation and fled ignominiously into the outer cold. A chill

◀ *What aspect of Buck's earlier life at the Judge's is contrasted? How has Buck's life changed?*

Words For Everyday Use

in • car • na • tion (in'kär nā'shən) *n.*, any person or thing that serves as an embodiment of a quality or concept
dis • com • fi • ture (dis kum'fi chər) *n.*, feeling of frustration and confusion

prow • ess (prou'is) *n.*, superior ability; skill
con • ster • na • tion (kän'stər nā'shen) *n.*, great fear or shock
ig • no • min • i • ous • ly (ig'nə min'ē əs lē) *adv.*, disgracefully; shamefully

wind was blowing that nipped him sharply and bit with especial venom into his wounded shoulder. He lay down on the snow and attempted to sleep, but the frost soon drove him shivering to his feet. Miserable and disconsolate, he wandered about among the many tents, only to find that one place was as cold as another. Here and there savage dogs rushed upon him, but he bristled his neck-hair and snarled (for he was learning fast), and they let him go his way unmolested.

Finally an idea came to him. He would return and see how his own teammates were making out. To his astonishment, they had disappeared. Again he wandered about through the great camp, looking for them, and again he returned. Were they in the tent? No, that could not be, else he would not have been driven out. Then where could they possibly be? With drooping tail and shivering body, very forlorn indeed, he aimlessly circled the tent. Suddenly the snow gave way beneath his forelegs and he sank down. Something wriggled under his feet. He sprang back, bristling and snarling, fearful of the unseen and unknown. But a friendly little yelp reassured him, and he went back to investigate. A whiff of warm air ascended to his nostrils, and there, curled up under the snow in a snug ball, lay Billee. He whined <u>placatingly</u>, squirmed and wriggled to show his good will and intentions, and even ventured, as a bribe for peace, to lick Buck's face with his warm wet tongue.

Another lesson. So that was the way they did it, eh? Buck confidently selected a spot, and with much fuss and wasted effort proceeded to dig a hole for himself. In a trice[2] the heat from his body filled the confined space and he was asleep. The day had been

---

2. **trice.** Very short time; moment

Words
For
Everyday
Use

pla • cat • ing • ly (plā´kāt´iŋ lē) *adv.,* pacifyingly; pleasingly

long and <u>arduous</u>, and he slept soundly and comfortably, though he growled and barked and wrestled with bad dreams.

Nor did he open his eyes till roused by the noises of the waking camp. At first he did not know where he was. It had snowed during the night and he was completely buried. The snow walls pressed him on every side, and a great surge of fear swept through him—the fear of the wild thing for the trap. It was a token that he was harking back through his own life to the lives of his <u>forebears</u>; for he was a civilized dog, an <u>unduly</u> civilized dog, and of his experience knew no trap and so could not of himself fear it. The muscles of his whole body contracted <u>spasmodically</u> and instinctively, the hair on his neck and shoulders stood on end, and with a ferocious snarl he bounded straight up into the blinding day, the snow flying about him in a flashing cloud. Ere he landed on his feet, he saw the white camp spread out before him and knew where he was and remembered all that had passed from the time he went for a stroll with Manuel to the hole he had dug for himself the night before.

◀ *What makes Buck afraid? What is the source of his fear?*

A shout from François hailed his appearance. "Wot I say?" the dog-driver cried to Perrault. "Dat Buck for sure learn queek as anyt'ing."

Perrault nodded gravely. As courier for the Canadian Government, bearing important dispatches, he was anxious to secure the best dogs, and he was particularly gladdened by the possession of Buck.

Three more huskies were added to the team inside an hour, making a total of nine, and before another quarter of an hour had passed they were in harness and swinging up the trail toward the Dyea Cañon. Buck was glad to be gone, and though the work was

---

Words For Everyday Use

ar • du • ous (är′jo͞o əs) *adj.*, strenuous; hard

fore • bear (fôr′ber′) *n.*, ancestor

un • du • ly (un do͞o′ē) *adv.*, excessively

spas • mod • i • cal • ly (spaz mäd′ik a lē) *adv.*, suddenly; violently; fitfully

hard he found he did not particularly despise it. He was surprised at the eagerness which animated the whole team and which was communicated to him; but still more surprising was the change wrought in Dave and Sol-leks. They were new dogs, utterly transformed by the harness. All passiveness and unconcern had dropped from them. They were alert and active, anxious that the work should go well, and fiercely irritable with whatever, by delay or confusion, retarded that work. The toil of the traces[3] seemed the supreme expression of their being, and all that they lived for and the only thing in which they took delight.

► How do the dogs feel when harnessed as a team?

Dave was wheeler or sled dog, pulling in front of him was Buck, then came Sol-leks; the rest of the team was strung out ahead, single file, to the leader, which position was filled by Spitz.

Buck had been purposely placed between Dave and Sol-leks so that he might receive instruction. Apt scholar that he was, they were equally apt teachers, never allowing him to linger long in error, and enforcing their teaching with their sharp teeth. Dave was fair and very wise. He never nipped Buck without cause, and he never failed to nip him when he stood in need of it. As François's whip backed him up, Buck found it to be cheaper to mend his ways than to retaliate. Once, during a brief halt, when he got tangled in the traces and delayed the start, both Dave and Sol-leks flew at him and administered a sound trouncing. The resulting tangle was even worse, but Buck took good care to keep the traces clear thereafter; and ere the day was done, so well had he mastered his work, his mates about ceased nagging him. François's whip snapped less frequently, and Perrault even honored Buck by lifting up his feet and carefully examining them.

► How are Buck's mistakes punished? How is his learning rewarded?

It was a hard day's run, up the Cañon, through Sheep Camp, past the Scales and the timberline,

---

3. **traces.** Straps and chains connecting a draft animal's harness to the vehicle drawn

across glaciers and snowdrifts hundreds of feet deep, and over the great Chilcoot Divide, which stands between the salt water and the fresh and guards forbiddingly the sad and lonely North. They made good time down the chain of lakes which fills the craters of extinct volcanoes, and late that night pulled into the huge camp at the head of Lake Bennett, where thousands of gold-seekers were building boats against the breakup of the ice in the spring. Buck made his hole in the snow and slept the sleep of the exhausted just, but all too early was <u>routed</u> out in the cold darkness and harnessed with his mates to the sled.

That day they made forty miles, the trail being packed; but the next day, and for many days to follow, they broke their own trail, worked harder, and made poorer time. As a rule, Perrault traveled ahead of the team, packing the snow with webbed shoes to make it easier for them. François, guiding the sled at the gee-pole,[4] sometimes exchanged places with him, but not often. Perrault was in a hurry, and he prided himself on his knowledge of ice, which knowledge was indispensable, for the fall ice was very thin, and where there was swift water, there was no ice at all.

Day after day, for days unending, Buck toiled in the traces. Always, they broke camp in the dark, and the first gray of dawn found them hitting the trail with fresh miles reeled off behind them. And always they pitched camp after dark, eating their bit of fish, and crawling to sleep into the snow. Buck was ravenous. The pound and a half of sun-dried salmon, which was his ration for each day, seemed to go nowhere. He never had enough, and suffered from perpetual hunger

---

4. **gee-pole.** Pole at the front of a dog sled for steering

rout (rout) *vt.*, make someone get out; force out

pangs. Yet the other dogs, because they weighed less and were born to the life, received a pound only of the fish and managed to keep in good condition.

He swiftly lost the <u>fastidiousness</u> which had characterized his old life. A dainty eater, he found that his mates, finishing first, robbed him of his unfinished ration. There was no defending it. While he was fighting off two or three, it was disappearing down the throats of the others. To remedy this, he ate as fast as they; and, so greatly did hunger compel him, he was not above taking what did not belong to him. He watched and learned. When he saw Pike, one of the new dogs, a clever <u>malingerer</u> and thief, slyly steal a slice of bacon when Perrault's back was turned, he duplicated the performance the following day, getting away with the whole chunk. A great uproar was raised, but he was unsuspected; while Dub, an awkward blunderer who was always getting caught, was punished for Buck's misdeed.

► What Northland virtue does Buck prove to possess?

This first theft marked Buck as fit to survive in the hostile Northland environment. It marked his adaptability, his capacity to adjust himself to changing conditions, the lack of which would have meant swift and terrible death. It marked, further, the decay or going to pieces of his moral nature, a vain thing and a handicap in the <u>ruthless</u> struggle for existence. It was all well enough in the Southland, under the law of love and fellowship, to respect private property and personal feelings; but in the Northland, under the law of club and fang, whoso took such things into account was a fool, and insofar as he observed them he would fail to prosper.

Not that Buck reasoned it out. He was fit, that was all, and unconsciously he accommodated himself to the new mode of life. All his days, no matter what

Words For Everyday Use

fas • ti • di • ous • ness (fas tid´ē əs nes) *n.*, oversensitiveness
ma • lin • ger • er (mə liŋ´gər ər) *n.*, someone who avoids duty
ruth • less (rōōth´lis) *adj.*, without pity

the odds, he had never run from a fight. But the club of the man in the red sweater had beaten into him a more fundamental and primitive code. Civilized, he could have died for a moral consideration, say the defense of Judge Miller's riding whip, but the completeness of his decivilization was now evidenced by his ability to flee from the defense of a moral consideration and so save his hide. He did not steal for joy of it, but because of the clamor of his stomach. He did not rob openly, but stole secretly and cunningly, out of respect for club and fang. In short, the things he did were done because it was easier to do them than not to do them.

◀ What new rules has Buck come to live by?

His development (or <u>retrogression</u>) was rapid. His muscles became hard as iron, and he grew callous to all ordinary pain. He achieved an internal as well as external economy. He could eat anything, no matter how loathsome or indigestible, and, once eaten, the juices of his stomach extracted the last least particle of nutriment; and his blood carried it to the farthest reaches of his body, building it into the toughest and stoutest of tissues. Sight and scent became remarkably keen, while his hearing developed such acuteness that in his sleep he heard the faintest sound and knew whether it <u>heralded</u> peace or peril. He learned to bite the ice out with his teeth when it collected between his toes; and when he was thirsty and there was a thick scum of ice over the water hole, he would break it by rearing and striking it with stiff fore legs. His most conspicuous trait was an ability to scent the wind and forecast it a night in advance. No matter how breathless the air when he dug his nest by tree or bank, the wind that later blew inevitably found him to leeward,[5] sheltered and snug.

---

5. **leeward.** Side or direction away from the wind

Words For Everyday Use	**re • tro • gres • sion** (re´trə gresh´ən) *n.*, return to a lower level or stage **her • ald** (her´əld) *v.*, announce; introduce

► Why does Buck learn so quickly?

And not only did he learn by experience, but instincts long dead became alive again. The domesticated generations fell from him. In vague ways he remembered back to the youth of the breed, to the time the wild dogs ranged in packs through the primeval forest and killed their meat as they ran it down. It was no task for him to learn to fight with cut and slash and the quick wolf snap. In this manner had fought forgotten ancestors. They quickened the old life within him, and the old tricks which they had stamped into the heredity of the breed were his tricks. They came to him without effort or discovery, as though they had been his always. And when, on the still cold nights, he pointed his nose at a star and howled long and wolflike, it was his ancestors, dead and dust, pointing nose at a star and howling down through the centuries and through him. And his <u>cadences</u> were their cadences, the cadences which voiced their woe and what to them was the meaning of the stillness, and the cold, and dark.

► What are the causes of Buck's self-discovery? How much control over these forces did Buck have?

Thus, as token of what a puppet thing life is, the ancient song surged through him and he came into his own again; and he came because men had found a yellow metal in the North, and because Manuel was a gardener's helper whose wages did not lap over the needs of his wife and <u>divers</u> small copies of himself.

Words For Everyday Use	ca • dence (kād´´ns) n., rhythmic flow of sound di • vers (dī´vərz) adj., several

Responding to the Selection

Imagine that you are Perrault. In your journal, write about the dog Buck, describing the changes in him that you see happening.

Reviewing the Selection

Recalling and Interpreting

1. **R:** What was Buck's first day on the Dyea beach like?
2. **I:** What event teaches Buck "the law of club and fang"?
3. **R:** How do the men react to the fight?
4. **I:** What is probably the reason that Buck feels toward Spitz "a bitter and deathless hatred"?
5. **R:** Where does Buck try to sleep his first night in camp? Where does he end up sleeping?
6. **I:** What action on Buck's part prompts François's exclamation, "Dat Buck for sure learn queek as anyt'ing"?
7. **R:** What action on Buck's part marks him as "fit to survive in the hostile Northland"?
8. **I:** Why is adaptability essential to survival?

Synthesizing

9. What is "the law of club and fang"?
10. What laws of the Southland are handicaps in the Northland? Why?

Understanding Literature

1. Character and Motive. A **character** is a person or animal who figures in the action of a story. A **motive** is a force that drives a character to act in a certain way. In this novel, the main character is an animal, the dog Buck. In this chapter, Buck develops a new behavior—stealing food. What motivates Buck to act in this way? What motive prevented him from acting this way in the past?

2. Theme. A **theme** is a central idea in a literary work. A long work such as a novel may deal with several interrelated themes. One of the themes in *The Call of the Wild* is the decivilization of Buck, a civilized creature who is placed in an uncivilized environment. What moral qualities does Buck shed in this chapter? Why are these qualities irrelevant, even dangerous, in an uncivilized environment such as the Northland?

CHAPTER III

The Dominant Primordial Beast

The dominant primordial beast was strong in Buck, and under the fierce conditions of trail life it grew and grew. Yet it was a secret growth. His newborn cunning gave him poise and control. He was too busy adjusting himself to the new life to feel at ease, and not only did he not pick fights, but he avoided them whenever possible. A certain deliberateness characterized his attitude. He was not prone to rashness and <u>precipitate</u> action; and in the bitter hatred between him and Spitz he betrayed no impatience, shunned all offensive acts.

On the other hand, possibly because he divined in Buck a dangerous rival, Spitz never lost an opportunity of showing his teeth. He even went out of his way to bully Buck, striving constantly to start the fight which could end only in the death of one or the other. Early in the trip this might have taken place had it not been for an unwonted accident. At the end of this day they made a bleak and miserable camp on the shore of Lake Le Barge. Driving snow, a wind that cut like a white-hot knife, and darkness had forced them to grope for a camping place. They could hardly have fared worse. At their backs rose a perpendicular wall of rock, and Perrault and François were compelled to make their fire and spread their sleeping robes on the ice of the lake itself. The tent they had discarded at Dyea in order to travel light. A few sticks of driftwood furnished them with a fire that thawed down through the ice and left them to eat supper in the dark.

◀ *What future events might be foreshadowed?*

◀ *What extra hardships do the dogs and their masters endure?*

Words For Everyday Use	pre • cip • i • tate (prē sip´ə tit) *adj.,* sudden; impetuous, rash

Close in under the sheltering rock Buck made his nest. So snug and warm was it that he was <u>loath</u> to leave it when François distributed the fish which he had first thawed over the fire. But when Buck finished his ration and returned, he found his nest occupied. A warning snarl told him that the trespasser was Spitz. Till now Buck had avoided trouble with his enemy, but this was too much. The beast in him roared. He sprang upon Spitz with a fury which surprised them both, and Spitz particularly, for his whole experience with Buck had gone to teach him that his rival was an unusually timid dog, who managed to hold his own only because of his great weight and size.

François was surprised, too, when they shot out in a tangle from the disrupted nest and he divined the cause of the trouble. "A-a-ah!" he cried to Buck. "Gif it to heem, by Gar! Gif it to heem, the dirty t'eef!"

Spitz was equally willing. He was crying with sheer rage and eagerness as he circled back and forth for a chance to spring in. Buck was no less eager, and no less cautious, as he likewise circled back and forth for the advantage. But it was then that the unexpected happened, the thing which projected their struggle for <u>supremacy</u> far into the future, past many a weary mile of trail and toil.

An oath from Perrault, the resounding impact of a club upon a bony frame, and a shrill yelp of pain, heralded the breaking forth of <u>pandemonium</u>. The camp was suddenly discovered to be alive with <u>skulking</u> furry forms—starving huskies, four or five score[1] of them, who had scented the camp from some Indian village. They had crept in while Buck and Spitz were fighting, and when the two men

▶ *Who attacks the camp? Why?*

---

1. **score.** Twenty people or things

sprang among them with stout clubs they showed their teeth and fought back. They were crazed by the smell of the food. Perrault found one with head buried in the grub-box.[2] His club landed heavily on the gaunt ribs, and the grub-box was capsized on the ground. On the instant a score of the famished brutes were scrambling for the bread and bacon. The clubs fell upon them unheeded. They yelped and howled under the rain of blows, but struggled nonetheless madly till the last crumb had been devoured.

In the meantime the astonished team dogs had burst out of their nests only to be set upon by the fierce invaders. Never had Buck seen such dogs. It seemed as though their bones would burst through their skins. They were mere skeletons, draped loosely in draggled hides, with blazing eyes and slavered fangs. But the hunger-madness made them terrifying, irresistible. There was no opposing them. The team dogs were swept back against the cliff at the first onset. Buck was beset by three huskies, and in a trice his head and shoulders were ripped and slashed. The din was frightful. Billee was crying as usual. Dave and Sol-leks, dripping blood from a score of wounds, were fighting bravely side by side. Joe was snapping like a demon. Once, his teeth closed on the foreleg of a husky, and he crunched down through the bone. Pike, the malingerer, leaped upon the crippled animal, breaking its neck with a quick flash of teeth and a jerk. Buck got a frothing adversary by the throat, and was sprayed with blood when his teeth sank through the jugular.[3] The warm taste of it in his mouth goaded him to greater fierceness. He flung

---

2. **grub-box.** Feed box
3. **jugular.** Large artery that delivers blood to the brain

Words
For
Everyday
Use

drag • gled (drag´əld) *adj.*, wet and dirty

himself upon another, and at the same time felt teeth sink into his own throat. It was Spitz, treacherously attacking from the side.

Perrault and François, having cleaned out their part of the camp, hurried to save their sled dogs. The wild wave of famished beasts rolled back before them, and Buck shook himself free. But it was only for a moment. The two men were compelled to run back to save the grub; upon which the huskies returned to the attack on the team. Billee, terrified into bravery, sprang through the savage circle and fled away over the ice. Pike and Dub followed on his heels, with the rest of the team behind. As Buck drew himself together to spring after them, out of the tail of his eye he saw Spitz rush upon him with the evident intention of overthrowing him. Once off his feet and under that mass of huskies, there was no hope for him. But he braced himself to the shock of Spitz's charge, then joined the flight out on the lake.

Later, the nine team dogs gathered together and sought shelter in the forest. Though unpursued, they were in a sorry plight. There was not one who was not wounded in four or five places, while some were wounded grievously. Dub was badly injured in a hind leg; Dolly, the last husky added to the team at Dyea, had a badly torn throat; Joe had lost an eye; while Billee, the good-natured, with an ear chewed and <u>rent</u> to ribbons, cried and whimpered throughout the night. At daybreak they limped <u>warily</u> back to camp, to find the <u>marauders</u> gone and the two men in bad tempers. Fully half their grub supply was gone. The huskies had chewed through the sled lashings and canvas coverings. In fact, nothing, no matter how remotely eatable, had escaped them. They had eaten a pair of Perrault's moosehide moccasins,

► *How does the team escape?*

Words For Everyday Use	**rent** (rent) *adj.,* torn **war • i • ly** (wer` ə lē) *adv.,* cautiously **ma • raud • er** (mə rôd´ər) *n.,* one who raids, pillages, or plunders

chunks out of the leather traces, and even two feet of lash from the end of François's whip. He broke from a mournful contemplation of it to look over his wounded dogs.

"Ah, my frien's," he said softly, "mebbe it mek you mad dog, dose many bites. Mebbe all mad dog, sacredam! Wot you t'ink, eh, Perrault?"

The courier shook his head <u>dubiously</u>. With four hundred miles of trail still between him and Dawson,[4] he could ill afford to have madness break out among his dogs. Two hours of cursing and <u>exertion</u> got the harnesses into shape, and the wound-stiffened team was under way, struggling painfully over the hardest part of the trail they had yet encountered, and for that matter, the hardest between them and Dawson.

The Thirty Mile River was wide open. Its wild water defied the frost, and it was in the <u>eddies</u> only and in the quiet places that the ice held at all. Six days of exhausting toil were required to cover those thirty terrible miles. And terrible they were, for every foot of them was accomplished at the risk of life to dog and man. A dozen times, Perrault, nosing the way, broke through the ice bridges, being saved by the long pole he carried, which he so held that it fell each time across the hole made by his body. But a cold snap was on, the thermometer registering fifty below zero, and each time he broke through he was compelled for very life to build a fire and dry his garments.

Nothing <u>daunted</u> him. It was because nothing daunted him that he had been chosen for government courier. He took all manner of risks, <u>resolutely</u>

◄ How does Perrault keep from falling through the ice? What does this reveal about his character?

---

4. **Dawson.** City in West Yukon, Canada, a base for gold miners

thrusting his little weazened face into the frost and struggling on from dim dawn to dark. He skirted the frowning shores on rim ice that bent and crackled under foot and upon which they dared not halt. Once, the sled broke through, with Dave and Buck, and they were half-frozen and all but drowned by the time they were dragged out. The usual fire was necessary to save them. They were coated solidly with ice, and the two men kept them on the run around the fire, sweating and thawing, so close that they were singed by the flames.

At another time Spitz went through, dragging the whole team after him up to Buck, who strained backward with all his strength, his forepaws on the slippery edge and the ice quivering and snapping all around. But behind him was Dave, likewise straining backward, and behind the sled was François, pulling till his tendons cracked.

Again, the rim ice broke away before and behind, and there was no escape except up the cliff. Perrault scaled it by a miracle, while François prayed for just that miracle; and with every thong and sled lashing and the last bit of harness rove[5] into a long rope, the dogs were hoisted, one by one, to the cliff crest. François came up last, after the sled and load. Then came the search for a place to descend, which descent was ultimately made by the aid of the rope, and night found them back on the river with a quarter of a mile to the day's credit.

By the time they made the Hootalinqua and good ice, Buck was played out. The rest of the dogs were in like condition; but Perrault, to make up lost time, pushed them late and early. The first day they covered thirty-five miles to the Big Salmon; the next day thirty-five more to the Little Salmon; the third day forty miles, which brought them well up toward the Five Fingers.[6]

---

5. **rove.** Woven
6. **Big Salmon . . . Little Salmon . . . Five Fingers.** Three rivers

Buck's feet were not so compact and hard as the feet of the huskies. His had softened during the many generations since the day his last wild ancestor was tamed by a cave dweller or river man. All day long he limped in agony, and camp once made, lay down like a dead dog. Hungry as he was, he would not move to receive his ration of fish, which François had to bring to him. Also, the dog-driver rubbed Buck's feet for half an hour each night after supper, and sacrificed the tops of his own moccasins to make four moccasins for Buck. This was a great relief, and Buck caused even the weazened face of Perrault to twist itself into a grin one morning, when François forgot the moccasins and Buck lay on his back, his four feet waving appealingly in the air, and refused to budge without them. Later his feet grew hard to the trail, and the worn-out footgear was thrown away.

◄ What disadvantage does Buck have? How does François help Buck?

At the Pelly one morning, as they were harnessing up, Dolly, who had never been conspicuous for anything, went suddenly mad. She announced her condition by a long, heartbreaking wolf howl that sent every dog bristling with fear, then sprang straight for Buck. He had never seen a dog go mad, nor did he have any reason to fear madness; yet he knew that here was horror, and fled away from it in a panic. Straight away he raced, with Dolly, panting and frothing, one leap behind; nor could she gain on him, so great was his terror, nor could he leave her, so great was her madness. He plunged through the wooded breast of the island, flew down to the lower end, crossed a back channel filled with rough ice to another island, gained a third island, curved back to the main river, and in desperation started to cross it. And all the time, though he did not look, he could hear her snarling just one leap behind. François called to him a quarter of a mile away and he doubled back, still one leap ahead, gasping painfully for air and putting all his faith in that François would save

◄ Why does Dolly chase Buck? What happens to her?

him. The dog-driver held the axe poised in his hand, and as Buck shot past him the axe crashed down upon mad Dolly's head.

Buck staggered over against the sled, exhausted, sobbing for breath, helpless. This was Spitz's opportunity. He sprang upon Buck, and twice his teeth sank into his unresisting foe and ripped and tore the flesh to the bone. Then François's lash descended, and Buck had the satisfaction of watching Spitz receive the worst whipping as yet administered to any of the team.

"One devil, dat Spitz," remarked Perrault. "Some dam day heem keel dat Buck."

"Dat Buck two devils," was François's rejoinder. "All de tam I watch dat Buck I know for sure. Lissen: some dam fine day heem get mad lak hell an' den heem chew dat Spitz all up an' spit heem out on de snow. Sure. I know."

From then on it was war between them. Spitz, as lead dog and acknowledged master of the team, felt his supremacy threatened by this strange Southland dog. And strange Buck was to him, for of the many Southland dogs he had known, not one had shown up worthily in camp and on trail. They were all too soft, dying under the toil, the frost, and starvation. Buck was the exception. He alone endured and prospered, matching the husky in strength, savagery, and cunning. Then he was a masterful dog, and what made him dangerous was the fact that the club of the man in the red sweater had knocked all blind pluck and rashness out of his desire for mastery. He was <u>preeminently</u> cunning, and could bide his time with a patience that was nothing less than primitive.

It was inevitable that the clash for leadership should come. Buck wanted it. He wanted it because

> ► How is Buck different from other Southland dogs? What makes Buck dangerous?

> ► Why does Buck want "the clash for leadership"?

Words For Everyday Use	**pre • em • i • nent • ly** (prē em´ə nənt lē) *adv.*, excelling above others

it was his nature, because he had been gripped tight by that nameless, incomprehensible pride of the trail and trace—that pride which holds dogs in the toil to the last gasp, which lures them to die joyfully in the harness, and breaks their hearts if they are cut out of the harness. This was the pride of Dave as wheel dog, of Sol-leks as he pulled with all his strength; the pride that laid hold of them at break of camp, transforming them from sour and sullen brutes into straining, eager, ambitious creatures; the pride that spurred them on all day and dropped them at pitch of camp at night, letting them fall back into gloomy unrest and uncontent. This was the pride that bore up Spitz and made him thrash the sled dogs who blundered and <u>shirked</u> in the traces or hid away at harness-up time in the morning. Likewise it was this pride that made him fear Buck as a possible lead dog. And this was Buck's pride, too.

He openly threatened the other's leadership. He came between him and the shirks he should have punished. And he did it deliberately. One night there was a heavy snowfall, and in the morning Pike, the malingerer, did not appear. He was securely hidden in his nest under a foot of snow. François called him and sought him in vain. Spitz was wild with wrath. He raged through the camp, smelling and digging in every likely place, snarling so frightfully that Pike heard and shivered in his hiding place.

But when he was at last unearthed, and Spitz flew at him to punish him, Buck flew, with equal rage, in between. So unexpected was it, and so shrewdly managed, that Spitz was hurled backward and off his feet. Pike, who had been trembling <u>abjectly</u>, took heart at this open <u>mutiny</u>, and sprang upon his overthrown leader. Buck, to whom fair play was a forgotten code, likewise sprang upon Spitz. But François, chuckling at the incident while unswerving in the administration of justice, brought his lash down upon Buck with all his might. This failed to drive Buck from his prostrate rival, and the butt of the whip was brought into play. Half stunned by the blow, Buck was knocked backward and the lash laid upon him again and again, while Spitz soundly punished the many times offending Pike.

In the days that followed, as Dawson grew closer and closer, Buck still continued to interfere between Spitz and the culprits; but he did it craftily, when François was not around. With the covert mutiny of Buck, a general insubordination sprang up and increased. Dave and Sol-leks were unaffected, but the rest of the team went from bad to worse. Things no longer went right. There was continual bickering and jangling. Trouble was always afoot, and at the bottom of it was Buck. He kept François busy, for the dog-driver was in constant apprehension of the life-and-death struggle between the two which he knew must take place sooner or later; and on more than one night the sounds of quarreling and strife among the other dogs turned him out of his sleeping robe, fearful that Buck and Spitz were at it.

But the opportunity did not present itself, and they pulled into Dawson one dreary afternoon with the great fight still to come. Here were many men, and countless dogs, and Buck found them all at work. It seemed the ordained order of things that dogs should work. All day they swung up and down the main street in long teams, and in the night their jingling bells still went by. They hauled cabin logs

Words For Everyday Use

pros • trate (präs´trāt´) adj., lying down
cov • ert (kuv´ərt) adj., concealed, hidden
or • dained (or dānd´) part., commanded

and firewood, freighted up to the mines, and did all manner of work that horses did in the Santa Clara Valley. Here and there Buck met Southland dogs, but in the main they were the wild wolf husky breed. Every night, regularly, at nine, at twelve, at three, they lifted a nocturnal song, a weird and eerie chant, in which it was Buck's delight to join.

With the aurora borealis[7] flaming coldly overhead, or the stars leaping in the frost dance, and the land numb and frozen under its <u>pall</u> of snow, this song of the huskies might have been the defiance of life, only it was pitched in minor key, with long-drawn wailings and half sobs, and was more the pleading of life, the articulate <u>travail</u> of existence. It was an old song, old as the breed itself—one of the first songs of the younger world in a day when songs were sad. It was invested with the woe of unnumbered generations, this plaint by which Buck was so strangely stirred. When he moaned and sobbed, it was with the pain of living that was of old the pain of his wild fathers, and the fear and mystery of the cold and dark that was to them fear and mystery. And that he should be stirred by it marked the completeness with which he harked back through the ages of fire and roof to the raw beginnings of life in the howling ages.

Seven days from the time they pulled into Dawson, they dropped down the steep bank by the Barracks to the Yukon Trail,[8] and pulled for Dyea and Salt Water. Perrault was carrying dispatches if anything more urgent than those he had brought in; also, the travel pride had gripped him, and he purposed to make the record trip of the year.

◄ Why do the dogs howl? What does their howling express?

◄ What does Perrault hope to accomplish? What things might help to make this goal possible?

---

7. **aurora borealis.** Luminous phenomena visible at night in a zone surrounding the north magnetic pole; northern lights
8. **Yukon Trail.** Trail running through Yukon Territory of Northwest Canada

Words For Everyday Use

pall (pôl) *n.,* covering
trav • ail (trə vāl´) *n.,* intense pain

Several things favored him in this. The week's rest had recuperated the dogs and put them in thorough trim. The trail they had broken into the country was packed hard by later journeyers. And further, the police had arranged in two or three places deposits of grub for dog and man, and he was traveling light.

They made Sixty Mile, which is a fifty-mile run, on the first day; and the second day saw them booming up the Yukon well on their way to Pelly. But such splendid running was achieved not without great trouble and vexation on the part of François. The insidious revolt led by Buck had destroyed the solidarity of the team. It no longer was as one dog leaping in the traces. The encouragement Buck gave the rebels led them into all kinds of petty misdemeanors. No more was Spitz a leader greatly to be feared. The old awe departed, and they grew equal to challenging his authority. Pike robbed him of half a fish one night, and gulped it down under the protection of Buck. Another night Dub and Joe fought Spitz and made him forego the punishment they deserved. And even Billee, the good-natured, was less good-natured, and whined not half so placatingly as in former days. Buck never came near Spitz without snarling and bristling menacingly. In fact, his conduct approached that of a bully, and he was given to swaggering up and down before Spitz's very nose.

The breaking down of discipline likewise affected the dogs in their relations with one another. They quarreled and bickered more than ever among themselves, till at times the camp was a howling bedlam. Dave and Sol-leks alone were unaltered, though they were made irritable by the unending squabbling. François swore strange barbarous oaths, and stamped the snow in futile rage, and tore his

► *What is happening to the dog team, and why?*

Words For Everyday Use

in • sid • i • ous (in sid´ē əs) *adj.,* sly or treacherous

sol • i • dar • i • ty (säl´ə dar´ə tē) *n.,* unity or agreement on an opinion or purpose

fu • tile (fyo͞ot´'l) *adj.,* useless; vain

hair. His lash was always singing among the dogs, but it was of small avail. Directly his back was turned they were at it again. He backed up Spitz with his whip, while Buck backed up the remainder of the team. François knew he was behind all the trouble, and Buck knew he knew; but Buck was too clever ever again to be caught red-handed. He worked faithfully in the harness, for the toil had become a delight to him; yet it was a greater delight slyly to precipitate a fight amongst his mates and tangle the traces.

◀ What does Buck enjoy?

At the mouth of the Tahkeena, one night after supper, Dub turned up a snowshoe rabbit, blundered it, and missed. In a second the whole team was in full cry. A hundred yards away was a camp of the Northwest Police, with fifty dogs, huskies all, who joined the chase. The rabbit sped down the river, turned off into a small creek, up the frozen bed of which it held steadily. It ran lightly on the surface of the snow, while the dogs ploughed through by main strength. Buck led the pack, sixty strong, around bend after bend, but he could not gain. He lay down low to the race, whining eagerly, his splendid body flashing forward, leap by leap, in the wan white moonlight. And leap by leap, like some pale frost wraith, the snowshoe rabbit flashed on ahead.

All that stirring of old instincts which at stated periods drives men out from the sounding cities to forest and plain to kill things by chemically propelled leaden pellets, the blood lust, the joy to kill— all this was Buck's, only it was infinitely more intimate. He was ranging at the head of the pack, running the wild thing down, the living meat, to kill with his own teeth and wash his muzzle to the eyes in warm blood.

Words For Everyday Use

pre • cip • i • tate (prē sip´ə tāt´) v., cause; start
wraith (rāth) n., ghost or specter

There is an ecstasy that marks the summit of life, and beyond which life cannot rise. And such is the paradox of living, this ecstasy comes when one is most alive, and it comes as a complete forgetfulness that one is alive. This ecstasy, this forgetfulness of living, comes to the artist, caught up and out of himself in a sheet of flame; it comes to the soldier, war-mad on a stricken field and refusing quarter; and it came to Buck, leading the pack, sounding the old wolf cry, straining after the food that was alive and that fled swiftly before him through the moonlight. He was sounding the deeps of his nature, and of the parts of his nature that were deeper than he, going back into the womb of Time. He was mastered by the sheer surging of life, the tidal wave of being, the perfect joy of each separate muscle, joint, and sinew in that it was everything that was not death, that it was aglow and rampant, expressing itself in movement, flying exultantly under the stars and over the face of dead matter that did not move.

But Spitz, cold and calculating even in his supreme moods, left the pack and cut across a narrow neck of land where the creek made a long bend around. Buck did not know of this, and as he rounded the bend, the frost wraith of a rabbit still flitting before him, he saw another and larger frost wraith leap from the overhanging bank into the immediate path of the rabbit. It was Spitz. The rabbit could not turn, and as the white teeth broke its back in midair it shrieked as loudly as a stricken man may shriek. At the sound of this, the cry of Life plunging down from Life's apex in the grip of Death, the full pack at Buck's heels raised a hell's chorus of delight.

Buck did not cry out. He did not check himself, but drove in upon Spitz, shoulder to shoulder, so

▶ What is Buck experiencing as he chases the rabbit?

▶ What has Spitz done? What does he hope to accomplish?

Words For Everyday Use

par • a • dox (par´ə däks´) n., person, situation, or act that seems to have contradictory, unbelievable, or absurd qualities
ram • pant (ram´pənt) adj., flourishing

ex • ult • ant • ly (eg zult´´nt lē) adv., triumphantly; rejoicingly
a • pex (ā´peks´) n., highest point

hard that he missed the throat. They rolled over and over in the powdery snow. Spitz gained his feet almost as though he had not been overthrown, slashing Buck down the shoulder and leaping clear. Twice his teeth clipped together, like the steel jaws of a trap, as he backed away for better footing, with lean and lifting lips that writhed and snarled.

In a flash Buck knew it. The time had come. It was to the death. As they circled about, snarling, ears laid back, keenly watchful for the advantage, the scene came to Buck with a sense of familiarity. He seemed to remember it all—the white woods, and earth, and moonlight, and the thrill of battle. Over the whiteness and silence brooded a ghostly calm. There was not the faintest whisper of air—nothing moved, not a leaf quivered, the visible breaths of the dogs rising slowly and lingering in the frosty air. They had made short work of the snowshoe rabbit, these dogs that were ill-tamed wolves; and they were now drawn up in an expectant circle. They, too, were silent, their eyes only gleaming and their breaths drifting slowly upward. To Buck it was nothing new or strange, this scene of old time. It was as though it had always been, the <u>wonted</u> way of things.

Spitz was a practiced fighter. From Spitzbergen through the Arctic, and across Canada and the Barrens, he had held his own with all manner of dogs and achieved to mastery over them. Bitter rage was his, but never blind rage. In passion to rend and destroy, he never forgot that his enemy was in like passion to rend and destroy. He never rushed till he was prepared to receive a rush; never attacked till he had first defended that attack.

In vain Buck strove to sink his teeth in the neck of the big white dog. Wherever his fangs struck for the

◀ *What does Buck realize as he begins to fight Spitz?*

◀ *What sense does Buck have about the fight?*

◀ *What had Spitz learned about fighting?*

Words For Everyday Use

wont • ed (wänt´ id) *adj.*, customary; habitual; usual

softer flesh, they were countered by the fangs of Spitz. Fang clashed fang, and lips were cut and bleeding, but Buck could not penetrate his enemy's guard. Then he warmed up and enveloped Spitz in a whirlwind of rushes. Time and time again he tried for the snow-white throat, where life bubbled near to the surface, and each time and every time Spitz slashed him and got away. Then Buck took to rushing, as though for the throat, when, suddenly drawing back his head and curving in from the side, he would drive his shoulder at the shoulder of Spitz, as a ram by which to overthrow him. But instead, Buck's shoulder was slashed down each time as Spitz leaped lightly away.

▶ What earlier event is recalled?

Spitz was untouched, while Buck was streaming with blood and panting hard. The fight was growing desperate. And all the while the silent and wolfish circle waited to finish off whichever dog went down. As Buck grew winded, Spitz took to rushing, and he kept him staggering for footing. Once Buck went over, and the whole circle of sixty dogs started up; but he recovered himself, almost in midair, and the circle sank down again and waited.

▶ What special quality does Buck possess?

But Buck possessed a quality that made for greatness—imagination. He fought by instinct, but he could fight by head as well. He rushed, as though attempting the old shoulder trick, but at the last instant swept low to the snow and in. His teeth closed on Spitz's left foreleg. There was a crunch of breaking bone, and the white dog faced him on three legs. Thrice he tried to knock him over, then repeated the trick and broke the right fore leg. Despite the pain and helplessness, Spitz struggled madly to keep up. He saw the silent circle, with gleaming eyes, lolling tongues, and silvery breaths drifting upward, closing in upon him as he had seen similar circles close in upon beaten antagonists in the past. Only this time he was the one who was beaten.

There was no hope for him. Buck was <u>inexorable</u>. Mercy was a thing reserved for gentler climes. He maneuvered for the final rush. The circle had tightened till he could feel the breaths of the huskies on his flanks. He could see them, beyond Spitz and to either side, half crouching for the spring, their eyes fixed upon him. A pause seemed to fall. Every animal was motionless as though turned to stone. Only Spitz quivered and bristled as he staggered back and forth, snarling with horrible menace, as though to frighten off <u>impending</u> death. Then Buck sprang in and out; but while he was in, shoulder had at last squarely met shoulder. The dark circle became a dot on the moon-flooded snow as Spitz disappeared from view. Buck stood and looked on, the successful champion, the dominant primordial beast who had made his kill and found it good.

◄ *How does Spitz behave in his final moments?*

Words For Everyday Use

in • ex • o • ra • ble (in eks´ə rə bəl) *adj.*, that which cannot be moved or influenced; unrelenting

im • pend • ing (im pend´iŋ) *part.*, about to happen; threatening

Responding to the Selection

In this chapter, Buck sheds the constraints of civilization and becomes a "primordial beast." What does it mean to be civilized? Why was Buck compelled to shed the constraints of civilization? Describe the characteristics of Buck, the "primordial beast."

Reviewing the Selection

Recalling and Interpreting

1. **R:** What primitive nature grows in Buck "under the fierce conditions of trail life"?

2. **I:** What action on the part of Spitz causes "the beast" in Buck to roar?

3. **R:** Who, or what, invades the camp?

4. **I:** What facts emphasize the "hunger madness" of these dogs?

5. **R:** What does Buck do when he hears the "nocturnal song" of the huskies in Dawson?

6. **I:** What qualities of the "nocturnal song" emphasize its connection to the ancient, "raw beginnings of life"?

7. **R:** What causes the breakdown of the solidarity of the sled team? Why does this happen?

8. **I:** What quality does Buck possess that ensures Spitz's fall from leadership?

Synthesizing

9. What instincts and characteristics does Buck, as a "dominant primordial beast," now possess?

10. What actions of the dogs, including Buck, are described as hereditary? What sort of relationship between heredity and survival is described in this chapter? How does Buck's fight with Spitz emphasize or exemplify that relationship?

Understanding Literature

1. Protagonist and **Antagonist.** A **protagonist,** or main character, is the central figure in a story. An **antagonist** is a character who is pitted against a protagonist. Which term describes the character Buck? Which describes Spitz? These characters are created primarily through the characterization techniques of direct description and portrayal of behavior. Compare and contrast the characteristics of Buck and Spitz. How are these characteristics displayed in the battles that eventually lead to the final fight to the death between Spitz and Buck?

2. Setting and **Mood.** The **setting** of a literary work is the time and place in which a story occurs, together with all the details used to create a sense of a particular time and place. The **mood** is the emotion created in the reader by descriptions of the setting, of characters, and of events. In the second paragraph of this chapter, what do the descriptions of the landscape and the weather tell about the conditions of the camp? What kind of mood is created by the description of the camp setting? How does this compare with the mood created by the description of daily life in Dawson?

CHAPTER IV

Who Has Won to Mastership

"Eh? Wot I say? I spik true w'en I say dat Buck two devils."

This was François's speech next morning when he discovered Spitz missing and Buck covered with wounds. He drew him to the fire and by its light pointed them out.

"Dat Spitz fight lak hell," said Perrault, as he surveyed the gaping rips and cuts.

"An' dat Buck fight lak two hells," was François's answer. "An' now we make good time. No more Spitz, no more trouble, sure."

While Perrault packed the camp outfit and loaded the sled, the dog-driver proceeded to harness the dogs. Buck trotted up to the place Spitz would have occupied as leader; but François, not noticing him, brought Sol-leks to the coveted position. In his judgment, Sol-leks was the best lead dog left. Buck sprang upon Sol-leks in a fury, driving him back and standing in his place.

"Eh? eh?" François cried, slapping his thighs gleefully. "Look at dat Buck. Heem keel dat Spitz, heem t'ink to take de job."

"Go 'way, Chook!" he cried, but Buck refused to budge.

He took Buck by the scruff of the neck, and though the dog growled threateningly, dragged him to one side and replaced Sol-leks. The old dog did not like it, and showed plainly that he was afraid of Buck. François was <u>obdurate</u>, but when he turned his back

► *What does Buck do to Sol-leks? Why?*

► *How does Sol-leks respond to Buck's threat?*

Words For Everyday Use

ob • du • rate (äb´do͞or it) *adj.*, not easily moved; stubborn

Buck again displaced Sol-leks, who was not at all unwilling to go.

François was angry. "Now, by Gar, I feex you!" he cried, coming back with a heavy club in his hand.

Buck remembered the man in the red sweater, and retreated slowly; nor did he attempt to charge in when Sol-leks was once more brought forward. But he circled just beyond the range of the club, snarling with bitterness and rage; and while he circled he watched the club so as to dodge it if thrown by François, for he was become wise in the way of clubs.

The driver went about his work, and he called to Buck when he was ready to put him in his old place in front of Dave. Buck retreated two or three steps. François followed him up, whereupon he again retreated. After some time of this, François threw down the club, thinking that Buck feared a thrashing. But Buck was in open revolt. He wanted, not to escape a clubbing, but to have the leadership. It was his by right. He had earned it, and he would not be content with less.

◄ *Why does Buck rebel?*

Perrault took a hand. Between them they ran him about for the better part of an hour. They threw clubs at him. He dodged. They cursed him, and his fathers and mothers before him, and all his seed to come after him down to the remotest generation, and every hair on his body and drop of blood in his veins; and he answered curse with snarl and kept out of their reach. He did not try to run away, but retreated around and around the camp, advertising plainly that when his desire was met, he would come in and be good.

François sat down and scratched his head. Perrault looked at his watch and swore. Time was flying, and they should have been on the trail an hour gone. François scratched his head again. He shook it and grinned sheepishly at the courier, who shrugged his shoulders in sign that they were beaten. Then François went up to where Sol-leks stood and called to Buck. Buck laughed, as dogs laugh, yet kept his distance. François unfastened Sol-leks's traces and put him back in his old place. The team stood harnessed to the sled in an unbroken line, ready for the trail. There was no place for Buck save at the front. Once more François called, and once more Buck laughed and kept away.

"T'row down de club," Perrault commanded.

François complied, whereupon Buck trotted in, laughing triumphantly, and swung around into position at the head of the team. His traces were fastened, the sled broken out, and with both men running they dashed out on to the river trail.

▶ *How does Buck act as lead dog? What qualities does he display?*

Highly as the dog-driver had forevalued Buck, with his two devils, he found, while the day was yet young, that he had undervalued. At a bound Buck took up the duties of leadership; and where judgment was required, and quick thinking and quick acting, he showed himself the superior even of Spitz, of whom François had never seen an equal.

But it was in giving the law and making his mates live up to it that Buck excelled. Dave and Sol-leks did not mind the change in leadership. It was none of their business. Their business was to toil, and toil mightily, in the traces. So long as that were not interfered with, they did not care what happened. Billee, the good-natured, could lead for all they cared, so long as he kept order. The rest of the team, however, had grown unruly during the last days of Spitz, and their surprise was great now that Buck proceeded to lick them into shape.

Pike, who pulled at Buck's heels, and who never put an ounce more of his weight against the breastband than he was compelled to do, was swiftly and repeatedly shaken for loafing; and ere the first day was done he was pulling more than ever before in his life. The first night in camp, Joe, the sour one, was punished roundly[1]—a thing that Spitz had never succeeded in doing. Buck simply smothered

---

1. **roundly.** Severely; fully

him by virtue of superior weight, and cut him up till he ceased snapping and began to whine for mercy.

The general tone of the team picked up immediately. It recovered its old-time solidarity, and once more the dogs leaped as one dog in the traces. At the Rink Rapids two native huskies, Teek and Koona, were added; and the <u>celerity</u> with which Buck broke them in took away François's breath.

◄ What happens to the dog team? What is the result of this change?

"Nevaire such a dog as dat Buck!" he cried. "No, nevaire! Heem worth one t'ousan' dollar, by Gar! Eh? Wot you say, Perrault?"

And Perrault nodded. He was ahead of the record then, and gaining day by day. The trail was in excellent condition, well packed and hard, and there was no new-fallen snow with which to contend. It was not too cold. The temperature dropped to fifty below zero and remained there the whole trip. The men rode and ran by turn, and the dogs were kept on the jump, with but infrequent stoppages.

The Thirty Mile River was comparatively coated with ice, and they covered in one day going out what had taken them ten days coming in. In one run they made a sixty-mile dash from the foot of Lake Le Barge to the White Horse Rapids. Across Marsh, Tagish, and Bennett (seventy miles of lakes), they flew so fast that the man whose turn it was to run towed behind the sled at the end of a rope. And on the last night of the second week they topped White Pass and dropped down the sea slope with the lights of Skaguay[2] and of the shipping at their feet.

It was a record run. Each day for fourteen days they had averaged forty miles. For three days Perrault and François threw chests up and down the

---

2. **Skaguay.** City in what is now Alaska that served as the entry point to the Yukon gold fields

Words For Everyday Use   ce • ler • i • ty (sə ler´i tē) n., swiftness

main street of Skaguay and were <u>deluged</u> with invitations to drink, while the team was the constant center of a worshipful crowd of dog-busters and mushers.[3] Then three or four western bad men <u>aspired</u> to clean out the town, were riddled like pepperboxes[4] for their pains, and public interest turned to other idols. Next came official orders. François called Buck to him, threw his arms around him, wept over him. And that was the last of François and Perrault. Like other men, they passed out of Buck's life for good.

► *How is the team's new work different from its prior work?*

A Scot took charge of him and his mates, and in company with a dozen other dog teams he started back over the weary trail to Dawson. It was no light running now, nor record time, but heavy toil each day, with a heavy load behind; for this was the mail train, carrying word from the world to the men who sought gold under the shadow of the Pole.

Buck did not like it, but he bore up well to the work, taking pride in it after the manner of Dave and Sol-leks, and seeing that his mates, whether they prided in it or not, did their fair share. It was a <u>monotonous</u> life, operating with machine-like regularity. One day was very like another. At a certain time each morning the cooks turned out, fires were built, and breakfast was eaten. Then, while some broke camp, others harnessed the dogs, and they were under way an hour or so before the darkness fell which gave warning of dawn. At night, camp was made. Some pitched the flies, others cut firewood and pine boughs for the beds, and still others carried water or ice for the cooks. Also, the dogs were fed. To

---

3. **dog-busters and mushers.** People who urge sled dogs to go faster
4. **pepperboxes.** Pepper shakers—containers with holes in the top for shaking out pepper

Words For Everyday Use

del • uge (del´ yo͞oj) *vi.,* overwhelm as with a flood
as • pire (əs pīr´) *vi.,* try, attempt; desire, aim
mo • not • o • nous (mə nät´n əs) *adj.,* unvarying; tiresome because unvarying

them, this was the one feature of the day, though it was good to loaf around, after the fish was eaten, for an hour or so with the other dogs, of which there were five score and odd. There were fierce fighters among them, but three battles with the fiercest brought Buck to mastery, so that when he bristled and showed his teeth they got out of his way.

Best of all, perhaps, he loved to lie near the fire, hind legs crouched under him, forelegs stretched out in front, head raised, and eyes blinking dreamily at the flames. Sometimes he thought of Judge Miller's big house in the sun-kissed Santa Clara Valley, and of the cement swimming-tank, and Ysabel, the Mexican hairless, and Toots, the Japanese pug; but oftener he remembered the man in the red sweater, the death of Curly, the great fight with Spitz, and the good things he had eaten or would like to eat. He was not homesick. The Sunland was very dim and distant, and such memories had no power over him. Far more <u>potent</u> were the memories of his <u>heredity</u> that gave things he had never seen before a seeming familiarity; the instincts (which were but the memories of his ancestors become habits) which had lapsed in later days, and still later, in him, quickened and became alive again.

◄ *What is important to Buck?*

Sometimes as he crouched there, blinking dreamily at the flames, it seemed that the flames were of another fire, and that as he crouched by this other fire he saw another and different man from the cook before him. This other man was shorter of leg and longer of arm, with muscles that were stringy and knotty rather than rounded and swelling. The hair of this man was long and matted, and his head slanted back under it from the eyes. He uttered strange sounds, and seemed very much afraid of the

◄ *Whom does Buck remember?*

Words For Everyday Use	po • tent (pōt´'nt) *adj.*, strong, powerful
	he • red • i • ty (hə red´i tē) *n.*, inherited characteristics

darkness, into which he peered continually, clutching in his hand, which hung midway between knee and foot, a stick with a heavy stone made fast to the end. He was all but naked, a ragged and fire-scorched skin hanging partway down his back, but on his body there was much hair. In some places, across the chest and shoulders and down the outside of the arms and thighs, it was matted into almost a thick fur. He did not stand erect, but with trunk inclined forward from the hips, on legs that bent at the knees. About his body there was a <u>peculiar</u> springiness, or <u>resiliency</u>, almost catlike, and a quick alertness as of one who lived in perpetual fear of things seen and unseen.

At other times this hairy man squatted by the fire with head between his legs and slept. On such occasions his elbows were on his knees, his hands clasped above his head as though to shed rain by the hairy arms. And beyond that fire, in the circling darkness, Buck could see many gleaming coals, two by two, always two by two, which he knew to be the eyes of great beasts of prey. And he could hear the crashing of their bodies through the undergrowth, and the noises they made in the night. And dreaming there by the Yukon bank, with lazy eyes blinking at the fire, these sounds and sights of another world would make the hair to rise along his back and stand on end across his shoulders and up his neck, till he whimpered low and <u>suppressedly</u>, or growled softly, and the cook shouted at him, "Hey, you Buck, wake up!" Whereupon the other world would vanish and the real world come into his eyes, and he would get up and yawn and stretch as though he had been asleep.

It was a hard trip, with the mail behind them, and the heavy work wore them down. They were short of weight and in poor condition when they made

Words For Everyday Use

pe • cu • liar (pə kyo͞ol´yər) *adj.,* unique, strange

re • sil • ien • cy (ri zil´yens ē) *n.,* ability to bounce or spring back to shape; ability to rebound

sup • pres • sed • ly (sə pres´ed lē) *adv.,* with restraint

Dawson, and should have had a ten days' or a week's rest at least. But in two days' time they dropped down the Yukon bank from the Barracks, loaded with letters for the outside. The dogs were tired, the drivers grumbling, and to make matters worse, it snowed every day. This meant a soft trail, greater friction on the runners, and heavier pulling for the dogs; yet the drivers were fair through it all, and did their best for the animals.

Each night the dogs were attended to first. They ate before the drivers ate, and no man sought his sleeping robe till he had seen to the feet of the dogs he drove. Still, their strength went down. Since the beginning of the winter they had traveled eighteen hundred miles, dragging sleds the whole weary distance; and eighteen hundred miles will tell upon life of the toughest. Buck stood it, keeping his mates up to their work and maintaining discipline, though he too was very tired. Billee cried and whimpered regularly in his sleep each night. Joe was sourer than ever, and Sol-leks was unapproachable, blind side or other side.

But it was Dave who suffered most of all. Something had gone wrong with him. He became more morose and irritable, and when camp was pitched at once made his nest, where his driver fed him. Once out of the harness and down, he did not get on his feet again till harness-up time in the morning. Sometimes, in the traces, when jerked by a sudden stoppage of the sled, or by straining to start it, he would cry out with pain. The driver examined him, but could find nothing. All the drivers became interested in his case. They talked it over at mealtime, and over their last pipes before going to bed, and one night they held a <u>consultation</u>. He was

◄ *What shows that something is wrong with Dave?*

brought from his nest to the fire and was pressed and prodded till he cried out many times. Something was wrong inside, but they could locate no broken bones, could not make it out.

By the time Cassiar Bar was reached, he was so weak that he was falling repeatedly in the traces. The Scot called a halt and took him out of the team, making the next dog, Sol-leks, fast to the sled. His intention was to rest Dave, letting him run free behind the sled. Sick as he was, Dave resented being taken out, grunting and growling while the traces were unfastened, and whimpering broken-heartedly when he saw Sol-leks in the position he had held and served so long. For the pride of trace and trail was his, and, sick unto death, he could not bear that another dog should do his work.

When the sled started, he <u>floundered</u> in the soft snow alongside the beaten trail, attacking Sol-leks with his teeth, rushing against him and trying to thrust him off into the soft snow on the other side, striving to leap inside his traces and get between him and the sled, and all the while whining and yelping and crying with grief and pain. The musher tried to drive him away with the whip; but he paid no heed to the stinging lash, and the man had not the heart to strike harder. Dave refused to run quietly on the trail behind the sled, where the going was easy, but continued to flounder alongside in the soft snow, where the going was most difficult, till exhausted. Then he fell, and lay where he fell, howling <u>lugubri-ously</u> as the long train of sleds churned by.

With the last remnant of his strength he managed to stagger along behind till the train made another stop, when he floundered past the sleds to his own, where he stood alongside Sol-leks. His driver lingered

▶ How does the Scot try to help Dave? How does Dave respond? Why does he respond in this way?

Words For Everyday Use

floun • der (floun´dər) vi., struggle awkwardly; stumble
lu • gu • bri • ous • ly (lə gōō´brē əs lē) adv., sadly, mournfully, often in an exaggerated manner

a moment to get a light for his pipe from the man behind. Then he returned and started his dogs. They swung out on the trail with remarkable lack of exertion, turned their heads uneasily, and stopped in surprise. The driver was surprised, too; the sled had not moved. He called his comrades to witness the sight. Dave had bitten through both of Sol-leks's traces, and was standing directly in front of the sled in his proper place.

◄ What does Dave want?

He pleaded with his eyes to remain there. The driver was perplexed. His comrades talked of how a dog could break its heart through being denied the work that killed it, and recalled instances they had known where dogs, too old for the toil, or injured, had died because they were cut out of the traces. Also, they held it a mercy, since Dave was to die anyway, that he should die in the traces, heart-easy and content. So he was harnessed in again, and proudly he pulled as of old, though more than once he cried out involuntarily from the bite of his inward hurt. Several times he fell down and was dragged in the traces, and once the sled ran upon him so that he limped thereafter in one of his hind legs.

But he held out till camp was reached, when his driver made a place for him by the fire. Morning found him too weak to travel. At harness-up time he tried to crawl to his driver. By <u>convulsive</u> efforts he got on his feet, staggered, and fell. Then he wormed his way forward slowly toward where the harnesses were being put on his mates. He would advance his forelegs and drag up his body with a sort of hitching movement, when he would advance his forelegs and hitch ahead again for a few more inches. His strength left him, and the last his mates saw of him he lay gasping in the snow and yearning toward

◄ What happens to Dave? Why does the Scot do this?

Words For Everyday Use	con • vul • sive (kən vul′siv) adj., occurring in violent fits; spasmodic

them. But they could hear him mournfully howling till they passed out of sight behind a belt of river timber.

Here the train was halted. The Scot slowly retraced his steps to the camp they had left. The men ceased talking. A revolver shot rang out. The man came back hurriedly. The whips snapped, the bells tinkled merrily, the sleds churned along the trail; but Buck knew, and every dog knew, what had taken place behind the belt of river trees.

Responding to the Selection

Imagine that you are François. Before heading out on your next official order, you have time to write a brief entry in your journal about the record run into Skaguay. Explain how you managed to average forty miles every day for fourteen days, expressing your feelings about having Buck as the lead dog.

Reviewing the Selection

Recalling and Interpreting

1. **R:** What position on the team does Buck think is his?

2. **I:** Which of Buck's actions show his ability to outsmart François and Perrault?

3. **R:** At what does Buck excel?

4. **I:** What actions show Buck's "mastership" over the other dogs?

5. **R:** What memories no longer hold any power over Buck?

6. **I:** What is probably the reason that "memories of his heredity" are becoming "far more potent" to Buck?

7. **R:** Which dog suffers most of all from the eighteen hundred miles traveled?

8. **I:** What actions on the part of Dave show his perseverance? What else do these actions show about Dave?

Synthesizing

9. Who is the other, "different" man in Buck's dream? How is this man described? What purpose is served by this description?

10. How do the dogs feel about pulling the sleds? What sort of relationship between a dog and his work is described in this chapter?

Understanding Literature

Character and Characterization. Characterization is the use of literary techniques to create a character. When using the characterization technique of portrayal of behavior, the writer presents the actions and speech of the character, allowing the reader to draw his or her own conclusions about the character from what the character says or does. The dog Dave is a **minor character**, a character who plays a lesser role in the action of the story. In this chapter, the character of Dave is described primarily through the portrayal of his behavior. What is revealed about Dave through his behavior? What qualities does he possess? For what qualities is he admired by the men and the rest of the dogs?

CHAPTER V

The Toil of Trace and Trail

Thirty days from the time it left Dawson, the Salt Water Mail, with Buck and his mates at the fore, arrived at Skaguay. They were in a wretched state, worn out and worn down. Buck's one hundred and forty pounds had dwindled to one hundred and fifteen. The rest of his mates, though lighter dogs, had relatively lost more weight than he. Pike, the malingerer, who, in his lifetime of deceit, had often successfully feigned a hurt leg, was now limping in earnest. Sol-leks was limping, and Dub was suffering from a wrenched shoulderblade.

They were all terribly footsore. No spring or rebound was left in them. Their feet fell heavily on the trail, jarring their bodies and doubling the fatigue of a day's travel. There was nothing the matter with them except that they were dead tired. It was not the dead-tiredness that comes through brief and excessive effort, from which recovery is a matter of hours; but it was the dead-tiredness that comes through the slow and prolonged strength drainage of months of toil. There was no power of recuperation left, no reserve strength to call upon. It had been all used, the last least bit of it. Every muscle, every fiber, every cell, was tired, dead tired. And there was reason for it. In less than five months they had traveled twenty-five hundred miles, during the last eighteen hundred of which they had had but five days' rest. When they arrived at Skaguay they were apparently on their last legs. They could barely keep the traces taut, and on the down grades just managed to keep out of the way of the sled.

"Mush on, poor sore feets," the driver encouraged them as they tottered down the main street of Skaguay. "Dis is de las'. Den we get one long res'. Eh? For sure. One bully long res'."

The drivers confidently expected a long stopover. Themselves, they had covered twelve hundred miles with two days' rest, and in the nature of reason and common justice they deserved an interval of loafing. But so many were the men who had rushed into the Klondike, and so many were the sweethearts, wives, and kin that had not rushed in, that the congested mail was taking on Alpine[1] proportions; also, there were official orders. Fresh batches of Hudson Bay dogs were to take the places of those worthless for the trail. The worthless ones were to be got rid of, and, since dogs count for little against dollars, they were to be sold.

Three days passed, by which time Buck and his mates found how really tired and weak they were. Then, on the morning of the fourth day, two men from the States came along and bought them, harness and all, for a song. The men addressed each other as "Hal" and "Charles." Charles was a middle-aged, lightish-colored man, with weak and watery eyes and a mustache that twisted fiercely and vigorously up, giving the lie to the limply drooping lip it concealed. Hal was a youngster of nineteen or twenty, with a big Colt's revolver and a hunting knife strapped about him on a belt that fairly bristled with cartridges. This belt was the most <u>salient</u> thing about him. It advertised his <u>callowness</u>— a callowness sheer and unutterable. Both men were <u>manifestly</u> out of place, and why such as they should adventure the

► What do the drivers expect? What thwarts their plans?

► What does Hal's belt say about him?

---

1. **Alpine.** Having the mountainous quality of the Alps, the highest mountains in Europe

Words For Everyday Use

sa • lient (sāl′yənt) adj., noticeable; prominent

cal • low • ness (kal′ō nes) n., youth; immaturity; state of being inexperienced

man • i • fest • ly (man′ə fest′lē) adv., clearly; obviously

North is part of the mystery of things that passes understanding.

Buck heard the chaffering,[2] saw the money pass between the man and the Government agent, and knew that the Scot and the mail-train drivers were passing out of his life on the heels of Perrault and François and the others who had gone before. When driven with his mates to the new owners' camp, Buck saw a slipshod and <u>slovenly</u> affair, tent half-stretched, dishes unwashed, everything in disorder; also, he saw a woman. "Mercedes" the men called her. She was Charles's wife and Hal's sister—a nice family party.

Buck watched them apprehensively as they proceeded to take down the tent and load the sled. There was a great deal of effort about their manner, but no businesslike method. The tent was rolled into an awkward bundle three times as large as it should have been. The tin dishes were packed away unwashed. Mercedes continually fluttered in the way of her men and kept up an unbroken chattering of <u>remonstrance</u> and advice. When they put a clothes sack on the front of the sled, she suggested it should go on the back; and when they had it put on the back, and covered it over with a couple of other bundles, she discovered overlooked articles which could abide nowhere else but in that very sack, and they unloaded again.

Three men from a neighboring tent came out and looked on, grinning and winking at one another.

"You've got a right smart load as it is," said one of them; "and it's not me should tell you your business, but I wouldn't tote that tent along if I was you."

◄ *Why is Buck apprehensive?*

---

2. **chaffering.** Bargaining, haggling over price

Words For Everyday Use

slov • en • ly (sluv´ən lē) *adj.,* careless; untidy; slipshod

re • mon • strance (ri män´strəns) *n.,* act of complaining, protesting

"Undreamed of!" cried Mercedes, throwing up her hands in dainty dismay. "However in the world could I manage without a tent?"

"It's springtime, and you won't get any more cold weather," the man replied.

She shook her head decidedly, and Charles and Hal put the last odds and ends on top of the mountainous load.

"Think it'll ride?" one of the men asked.

"Why shouldn't it?" Charles demanded rather shortly.

"Oh, that's all right, that's all right," the man hastened meekly to say. "I was just a-wonderin', that is all. It seemed a mite top-heavy."

Charles turned his back and drew the lashings down as well as he could, which was not in the least well.

"An' of course the dogs can hike along all day with that contraption behind them," affirmed a second of the men.

"Certainly," said Hal, with freezing politeness, taking hold of the gee-pole with one hand and swinging his whip from the other. "Mush!" he shouted. "Mush on there!"

The dogs sprang against the breastbands, strained hard for a few moments, then relaxed. They were unable to move the sled.

"The lazy brutes, I'll show them," he cried, preparing to lash out at them with the whip.

But, Mercedes interfered, crying, "Oh, Hal, you mustn't," as she caught hold of the whip and wrenched it from him. "The poor dears! Now you must promise you won't be harsh with them for the rest of the trip, or I won't go a step."

"Precious lot you know about dogs," her brother sneered; "and I wish you'd leave me alone. They're lazy, I tell you, and you've got to whip them to get anything out of them. That's their way. You ask any one. Ask one of those men."

▶ Why does Hal sneer at Mercedes? Does he know any more about dogs than she does? How do you know this?

Mercedes looked at them imploringly, untold repugnance at sight of pain written in her pretty face.

"They're weak as water, if you want to know," came the reply from one of the men. "Plum tuckered out, that's what's the matter. They need a rest."

"Rest be blanked," said Hal, with his beardless lips; and Mercedes said, "Oh!" in pain and sorrow at the oath.

But she was a clannish creature, and rushed at once to the defense of her brother. "Never mind that man," she said pointedly. "You're driving our dogs, and you do what you think best with them."

◄ Why does Mercedes defend Hal even though doing so contradicts her earlier plea?

Again Hal's whip fell upon the dogs. They threw themselves against the breastbands, dug their feet into the packed snow, got down low to it, and put forth all their strength. The sled held as though it were an anchor. After two efforts, they stood still, panting. The whip was whistling savagely, when once more Mercedes interfered. She dropped on her knees before Buck, with tears in her eyes, and put her arms around his neck.

"You poor, poor dears," she cried sympathetically, "why don't you pull hard? Then you wouldn't be whipped." Buck did not like her, but he was feeling too miserable to resist her, taking it as part of the day's miserable work.

One of the onlookers, who had been clenching his teeth to suppress hot speech, now spoke up:—

"It's not that I care a whoop what becomes of you, but for the dogs' sakes I just want to tell you, you can help them a mighty lot by breaking out that sled. The runners are froze fast. Throw your weight against the gee-pole, right and left, and break it out."

Words For Everyday Use   re • pug • nance (ri pug′nəns) *n.*, extreme dislike or distaste

▶ Why does the sled overturn? Why does the load spill? What predictions can you make about the rest of the trip based on this information?

A third time the attempt was made, but this time, following the advice, Hal broke out the runners which had been frozen to the snow. The overloaded and unwieldy sled forged ahead, Buck and his mates struggling frantically under the rain of blows. A hundred yards ahead the path turned and sloped steeply into the main street. It would have required an experienced man to keep the top-heavy sled upright, and Hal was not such a man. As they swung on the turn the sled went over, spilling half its load through the loose lashings. The dogs never stopped. The lightened sled bounded on its side behind them. They were angry because of the ill treatment they had received and the unjust load. Buck was raging. He broke into a run, the team following his lead. Hal cried "Whoa! whoa!" but they gave no heed. He tripped and was pulled off his feet. The capsized sled ground over him, and the dogs dashed on up the street, adding to the gaiety of Skaguay as they scattered the remainder of the outfit along its chief thoroughfare.

Kindhearted citizens caught the dogs and gathered up the scattered belongings. Also, they gave advice. Half the load and twice the dogs if they ever expected to reach Dawson, was what was said. Hal and his sister and brother-in-law listened unwillingly, pitched tent, and overhauled the outfit. Canned goods were turned out that made men laugh, for canned goods on the Long Trail is a thing to dream about. "Blankets for a hotel," quoth one of the men who laughed and helped. "Half as many is too much; get rid of them. Throw away that tent, and all those dishes, who's going to wash them, anyway? Good Lord, do you think you're traveling on a Pullman?"[3]

▶ What kinds of things did the inexperienced sledders pack? What factors did they consider when packing?

---

3. **Pullman.** Railroad passenger car with convertible berths for sleeping

And so it went, the inexorable elimination of the superfluous. Mercedes cried when her clothes bags were dumped on the ground and article after article was thrown out. She cried in general, and she cried in particular over each discarded thing. She clasped hands about knees, rocking back and forth broken-heartedly. She averred she would not go an inch, not for a dozen Charleses. She appealed to everybody and to everything, finally wiping her eyes and pro-ceeding to cast out even articles of apparel that were imperative necessaries. And in her zeal, when she had finished with her own, she attacked the belong-ings of her men and went through them like a tor-nado.

This accomplished, the outfit, though cut in half, was still a formidable bulk. Charles and Hal went out in the evening and bought six Outside dogs. These, added to the six of the original team, and Teek and Koona, the huskies obtained at the Rink Rapids on the record trip, brought the team up to fourteen. But the Outside dogs, though practically broken in since their landing, did not amount to much. Three were short-haired pointers, one was a Newfoundland, and the other two were mongrels of indeterminate breed. They did not seem to know anything, these newcomers. Buck and his comrades looked upon them with disgust, and though he speedily taught them their places and what not to do, he could not teach them what to do. They did not take kindly to trace and trail. With the exception of the two mon-grels, they were bewildered and spirit-broken by the strange savage environment in which they found themselves and by the ill treatment they had received. The two mongrels were without spirit at

Words
For
Everyday
Use

su • per • flu • ous (sə pur´floo əs) *adj.*, being more than is needed, excessive

a • ver (ə vur´) *vt.*, declare to be true, affirm

for • mi • da • ble (fôr´mə də bəl) *adj.*, large; hard to handle

all; bones were the only things breakable about them.

With the newcomers hopeless and forlorn, and the old team worn out by twenty-five hundred miles of continuous trail, the outlook was anything but bright. The two men, however, were quite cheerful. And they were proud, too. They were doing the thing in style, with fourteen dogs. They had seen other sleds depart over the Pass for Dawson, or come in from Dawson, but never had they seen a sled with so many as fourteen dogs. In the nature of Arctic travel there was a reason why fourteen dogs should not drag one sled, and that was that one sled could not carry the food for fourteen dogs. But Charles and Hal did not know this. They had worked the trip out with a pencil, so much to a dog, so many dogs, so many days, Q.E.D.[4] Mercedes looked over their shoulders and nodded comprehensively, it was all so very simple.

► Why had Hal and Charles never seen a sled with fourteen dogs?

Late next morning Buck led the long team up the street. There was nothing lively about it, no snap or go in him and his fellows. They were starting dead weary. Four times he had covered the distance between Salt Water and Dawson, and the knowledge that, jaded and tired, he was facing the same trail once more, made him bitter. His heart was not in the work, nor was the heart of any dog. The Outsides were timid and frightened, the Insides without confidence in their masters.

► How are the dogs feeling as they set out? Why is Buck's feeling justified?

Buck felt vaguely that there was no depending upon these two men and the woman. They did not know how to do anything, and as the days went by it became apparent that they could not learn. They

---

4. Q.E.D. Latin, *quod erat demonstrandum*; which was to be demonstrated or proved

Words For Everyday Use

jad • ed (jād´id) *adj.,* worn out; dulled

were slack in all things, without order or discipline. It took them half the night to pitch a slovenly camp, and half the morning to break that camp and get the sled loaded in fashion so slovenly that for the rest of the day they were occupied in stopping and rearranging the load. Some days they did not make ten miles. On other days they were unable to get started at all. And on no day did they succeed in making more than half the distance used by the men as a basis in their dog food computation.

It was inevitable that they should go short on dog food. But they hastened it by overfeeding, bringing the day nearer when underfeeding would commence. The Outside dogs, whose digestions had not been trained by chronic famine to make the most of little, had <u>voracious</u> appetites. And when, in addition to this, the worn-out huskies pulled weakly, Hal decided that the <u>orthodox</u> ration was too small. He doubled it. And to cap it all, when Mercedes, with tears in her pretty eyes and a quaver in her throat, could not cajole him into giving the dogs still more, she stole from the fish sacks and fed them slyly. But it was not food that Buck and the huskies needed, but rest. And though they were making poor time, the heavy load they dragged sapped their strength severely.

Then came the underfeeding. Hal awoke one day to the fact that his dog food was half gone and the distance only quarter covered; further, that for love or money no additional dog food was to be obtained. So he cut down even the orthodox ration and tried to increase the day's travel. His sister and brother-in-law seconded him; but they were frustrated by their heavy outfit and their own <u>incompetence.</u> It was a simple matter to give the dogs less

◄ *What did the people do to cause food supply problems?*

◄ *How does Hal try to remedy the problem? Why doesn't this solution work?*

Words
For
Everyday
Use

vo • ra • cious (vô rā´shəs) *adj.,* greedy; ravenous
or • tho • dox (ôr´thō däks´) *adj.,* usual; established (as in beliefs)
in • com • pe • tence (in käm´pə təns) *n.,* lack of ability or skill

food; but it was impossible to make the dogs travel faster, while their own inability to get under way earlier in the morning prevented them from traveling longer hours. Not only did they not know how to work dogs, but they did not know how to work themselves.

The first to go was Dub. Poor blundering thief that he was, always getting caught and punished, he had nonetheless been a faithful worker. His wrenched shoulder blade, untreated and unrested, went from bad to worse, till finally Hal shot him with the big Colt's revolver. It is a saying of the country that an Outside dog starves to death on the ration of the husky, so the six Outside dogs under Buck could do no less than die on half the ration of the husky. The Newfoundland went first, followed by the three short-haired pointers, the two mongrels hanging more grittily on to life, but going in the end.

By this time all the <u>amenities</u> and gentlenesses of the Southland had fallen away from the three people. Shorn of its glamour and romance, Arctic travel became to them a reality too harsh for their manhood and womanhood. Mercedes ceased weeping over the dogs, being too occupied with weeping over herself and with quarreling with her husband and brother. To quarrel was the one thing they were never too weary to do. Their irritability arose out of their misery, increased with it, doubled upon it, outdistanced it. The wonderful patience of the trail which comes to men who toil hard and suffer sore, and remain sweet of speech and kindly, did not come to these two men and the woman. They had no inkling of such a patience. They were stiff and in pain; their muscles ached, their bones ached, their very hearts ached; and because of this they became sharp of

▶ How do Charles, Hal, and Mercedes react to life on the trail?

Words For Everyday Use

a • men • i • ty (ə menˊə tē) *n.,* comfort or convenience

speech, and hard words were first on their lips in the morning and last at night.

Charles and Hal <u>wrangled</u> whenever Mercedes gave them a chance. It was the cherished belief of each that he did more than his share of the work, and neither forbore to speak this belief at every opportunity. Sometimes Mercedes sided with her husband, sometimes with her brother. The result was a beautiful and unending family quarrel. Starting from a dispute as to which should chop a few sticks for the fire (a dispute which concerned only Charles and Hal), presently would be lugged in the rest of the family, fathers, mothers, uncles, cousins, people thousands of miles away, and some of them dead. That Hal's views on art, or the sort of society plays his mother's brother wrote, should have anything to do with the chopping of a few sticks of firewood, passes comprehension; nevertheless the quarrel was as likely to tend in that direction as in the direction of Charles's political prejudices. And that Charles's sister's tale-bearing tongue should be relevant to the building of a Yukon fire was apparent only to Mercedes, who disburdened herself of <u>copious</u> opinions upon that topic, and incidentally upon a few other traits unpleasantly peculiar to her husband's family. In the meantime the fire remained unbuilt, the camp half pitched, and the dogs unfed.

Mercedes nursed a special grievance—the grievance of sex. She was pretty and soft, and had been chivalrously treated all her days. But the present treatment by her husband and brother was everything save chivalrous. It was her custom to be helpless. They complained. Upon which <u>impeachment</u> of what to her was her most essential sex-<u>prerogative</u>, she made their lives unendurable. She no longer considered the dogs, and because she was

Words For Everyday Use	**wran • gle** (raŋ´gəl) *vi.*, quarrel angrily and noisily	**im • peach • ment** (im pēch´ment) *n.*, discredit
	co • pi • ous (kō´pē əs) *adj.*, numerous, many	**pre • rog • a • tive** (prē räg´ə tiv) *n.*, right or privilege, especially peculiar to a rank or class

sore and tired, she persisted in riding on the sled. She was pretty and soft, but she weighed one hundred and twenty pounds—a lusty last straw to the load dragged by the weak and starving animals. She rode for days, till they fell in the traces and the sled stood still. Charles and Hal begged her to get off and walk, pleaded with her, entreated, the while she wept and <u>importuned</u> Heaven with a recital of their brutality.

On one occasion they took her off the sled by main strength. They never did it again. She let her legs go limp like a spoiled child, and sat down on the trail. They went on their way, but she did not move. After they had traveled three miles they unloaded the sled, came back for her, and by main strength put her on the sled again.

In the excess of their own misery they were <u>callous</u> to the suffering of their animals. Hal's theory, which he practiced on others, was that one must get hardened. He had started out preaching it to his sister and brother-in-law. Failing there, he hammered it into the dogs with a club. At the Five Fingers the dog food gave out, and a toothless old squaw offered to trade them a few pounds of frozen horsehide for the Colt's revolver that kept the big hunting knife company at Hal's hip. A poor substitute for food was this hide, just as it had been stripped from the starved horses of the cattlemen six months back. In its frozen state it was more like strips of galvanized iron, and when a dog wrestled it into his stomach it thawed into thin and innutritious leathery strings and into a mass of short hair, irritating and indigestible.

And through it all Buck staggered along at the head of the team as in a nightmare. He pulled when

► What is Hal's theory? To whom is he unable to teach this lesson? To whom does he teach it instead?

Words For Everyday Use

im • por • tune (im´pôr toon´) vt., trouble with requests or demands

cal • lous (kal´əs) adj., unfeeling

he could; when he could no longer pull, he fell down and remained down till blows from whip or club drove him to his feet again. All the stiffness and gloss had gone out of his beautiful furry coat. The hair hung down, limp and draggled, or matted with dried blood where Hal's club had bruised him. His muscles had wasted away to knotty strings, and the flesh pads had disappeared, so that each rib and every bone in his frame were outlined cleanly through the loose hide that was wrinkled in folds of emptiness. It was heartbreaking, only Buck's heart was unbreakable. The man in the red sweater had proved that.

As it was with Buck, so was it with his mates. They were <u>perambulating</u> skeletons. There were seven all together, including him. In their very great misery they had become insensible to the bite of the lash or the bruise of the club. The pain of the beating was dull and distant, just as the things their eyes saw and their ears heard seemed dull and distant. They were not half living, or quarter living. They were simply so many bags of bones in which sparks of life fluttered faintly. When a halt was made, they dropped down in the traces like dead dogs, and the spark dimmed and paled and seemed to go out. And when the club or whip fell upon them, the spark fluttered feebly up, and they tottered to their feet and staggered on.

There came a day when Billee, the good-natured, fell and could not rise. Hal had traded off his revolver, so he took the axe and knocked Billee on the head as he lay in the traces, then cut the carcass out of the harness and dragged it to one side. Buck saw, and his mates saw, and they knew that this thing was very close to them. On the next day

◀ *What has happened to the dogs since this journey began?*

| Words For Everyday Use | per • am • bu • late (pər am´byo͞o lāt´) *vi.*, walk about |

Koona went, and but five of them remained: Joe, too far gone to be malignant; Pike, crippled and limping, only half conscious and not conscious enough longer to malinger; Sol-leks, the one-eyed, still faithful to the toil of trace and trail, and mournful in that he had so little strength with which to pull; Teek, who had not traveled so far that winter and who was now beaten more than the others because he was fresher; and Buck, still at the head of the team, but no longer enforcing discipline or striving to enforce it, blind with weakness half the time and keeping the trail by the loom of it and by the dim feel of his feet.

It was beautiful spring weather, but neither dogs nor humans were aware of it. Each day the sun rose earlier and set later. It was dawn by three in the morning, and twilight lingered till nine at night. The whole long day was a blaze of sunshine. The ghostly winter silence had given way to the great spring murmur of awakening life. This murmur arose from all the land, <u>fraught</u> with the joy of living. It came from the things that lived and moved again, things which had been as dead and which had not moved during the long months of frost. The sap was rising in the pines. The willows and aspens were bursting out in young buds. Shrubs and vines were putting on fresh garbs of green. Crickets sang in the nights, and in the days all manner of creeping, crawling things rustled forth into the sun. Partridges and woodpeckers were booming and knocking in the forest. Squirrels were chattering, birds singing, and overhead honked the wild fowl driving up from the south in cunning wedges that split the air.

▶ *How does this picture of the spring landscape contrast with the portrait of the travelers?*

Words For Everyday Use	**fraught** (frôt) *adj.*, filled; charged; loaded

From every hill slope came the trickle of running water, the music of unseen fountains. All things were thawing, bending, snapping. The Yukon was straining to break loose the ice that bound it down. It ate away from beneath; the sun ate from above. Air holes formed, fissures sprang and spread apart, while thin sections of ice fell through bodily into the river. And amid all this bursting, rending, throbbing of awakening life, under the blazing sun and through the soft-sighing breezes, like wayfarers to death, staggered the two men, the woman, and the huskies.

With the dogs falling, Mercedes weeping and riding, Hal swearing <u>innocuously</u>, and Charles's eyes wistfully watering, they staggered into John Thornton's camp at the mouth of White River. When they halted, the dogs dropped down as though they had all been struck dead. Mercedes dried her eyes and looked at John Thornton. Charles sat down on a log to rest. He sat down very slowly and painstakingly, what of his great stiffness. Hal did the talking. John Thornton was whittling the last touches on an axe-handle he had made from a stick of birch. He whittled and listened, gave monosyllabic[5] replies, and, when it was asked, <u>terse</u> advice. He knew the breed, and he gave his advice in the certainty that it would not be followed.

◄ *What does John Thornton recognize about the characters of these people?*

"They told us up above that the bottom was dropping out of the trail and that the best thing for us to do was to lay over," Hal said in response to Thornton's warning to take no more chances on the rotten ice. "They told us we couldn't make White River, and here we are." This last with a sneering ring of triumph in it.

---

5. **monosyllabic.** Having only one syllable

Words For Everyday Use

in • no • cu • ous • ly (in näk´yo͞o əs lē) *adv.*, harmlessly; dully

terse (tɥrs) *adj.*, short; concise

▶ What answer does Thornton give to Hal's triumphant sneer? What advice does Thornton give?

"And they told you true," John Thornton answered. "The bottom's likely to drop out at any moment. Only fools, with the blind luck of fools, could have made it. I tell you straight, I wouldn't risk my carcass on that ice for all the gold in Alaska."

"That's because you're not a fool, I suppose," said Hal. "All the same, we'll go on to Dawson." He uncoiled his whip. "Get up there, Buck! Hi! Get up there! Mush on!"

Thornton went on whittling. It was idle, he knew, to get between a fool and his folly, while two or three fools more or less would not alter the scheme of things.

But the team did not get up at the command. It had long since passed into the stage where blows were required to rouse it. The whip flashed out, here and there, on its merciless errands. John Thornton compressed his lips. Sol-leks was the first to crawl to his feet. Teek followed. Joe came next, yelping with pain. Pike made painful efforts. Twice he fell over, when half up, and on the third attempt managed to rise. Buck made no effort. He lay quietly where he had fallen. The lash bit into him again and again, but he neither whined nor struggled. Several times Thornton started, as though to speak, but changed his mind. A moisture came into his eyes, and, as the whipping continued, he arose and walked <u>irresolutely</u> up and down.

▶ What does Buck do for the first time? Why is he different from his mates?

This was the first time Buck had failed, in itself a sufficient reason to drive Hal into a rage. He exchanged the whip for the customary club. Buck refused to move under the rain of heavier blows which now fell upon him. Like his mates, he was barely able to get up, but, unlike them, he had made up his mind not to get up. He had a vague

Words For Everyday Use

ir • re • so • lute • ly (ir rez´ə lo͞ot´lē) *adv.,* indecisively feeling of impending doom. This had been strong upon him when he pulled in to the bank, and it had not departed from him. What of the thin and rotten ice he had felt under his feet all day, it seemed that he sensed disaster close at hand, out there ahead on the ice where his master was trying to drive him. He refused to stir. So greatly had he suffered, and so far gone was he, that the blows did not hurt much. And as they continued to fall upon him, the spark of life within flickered and went down. It was nearly out. He felt strangely numb. As though from a great distance, he was aware that he was being beaten. The last sensations of pain left him. He no longer felt anything, though very faintly he could hear the impact of the club upon his body. But it was no longer his body, it seemed so far away.

And then, suddenly, without warning, uttering a cry that was <u>inarticulate</u> and more like the cry of an animal, John Thornton sprang upon the man who wielded the club. Hal was hurled backward, as though struck by a falling tree. Mercedes screamed. Charles looked on wistfully, wiped his watery eyes, but did not get up because of his stiffness.

John Thornton stood over Buck, struggling to control himself, too convulsed with rage to speak.

"If you strike that dog again, I'll kill you," he at last managed to say in a choking voice.

"It's my dog," Hal replied, wiping the blood from his mouth as he came back. "Get out of my way, or I'll fix you. I'm going to Dawson."

Thornton stood between him and Buck, and <u>evinced</u> no intention of getting out of the way. Hal drew his long hunting-knife. Mercedes screamed, cried, laughed, and manifested the chaotic abandonment of

Words
For
Everyday
Use

in • ar • tic • u • late (in´är tik´yōō lit) *adj.*, incomprehensible, not understandable

e • vince (ē vins´) *vt.*, show plainly; indicate

hysteria. Thornton rapped Hal's knuckles with the axe-handle, knocking the knife to the ground. He rapped his knuckles again as he tried to pick it up. Then he stooped, picked it up himself, and with two strokes cut Buck's traces.

▶ What three reasons does Hal have for giving up Buck?

Hal had no fight left in him. Besides, his hands were full with his sister, or his arms, rather; while Buck was too near dead to be of further use in hauling the sled. A few minutes later they pulled out from the bank and down the river. Buck heard them go and raised his head to see. Pike was leading, Sol-leks was at the wheel, and between were Joe and Teek. They were limping and staggering. Mercedes was riding the loaded sled. Hal guided at the gee-pole, and Charles stumbled along in the rear.

As Buck watched them, Thornton knelt beside him and with rough, kindly hands searched for broken bones. By the time his search had disclosed nothing more than many bruises and a state of terrible starvation, the sled was a quarter of a mile away. Dog and man watched it crawling along over the ice.

▶ What happens to the sled? Do you feel sympathy for Charles, Mercedes, and Hal when this happens? Why, or why not?

Suddenly, they saw its back end drop down, as into a rut, and the gee-pole, with Hal clinging to it, jerk into the air. Mercedes's scream came to their ears. They saw Charles turn and make one step to run back, and then a whole section of ice give way and dogs and humans disappear. A yawning hole was all that was to be seen. The bottom had dropped out of the trail.

John Thornton and Buck looked at each other.

"You poor devil," said John Thornton, and Buck licked his hand.

Responding to the Selection

Imagine that you are John Thornton. In your journal, write about Buck, explaining why you saved his life. Express your feelings about Hal in your journal entry.

Reviewing the Selection

Recalling and Interpreting

1. **R:** In what condition are the dogs when they reach Skaguay?

2. **I:** What facts emphasize the grueling effects of the trail upon the dogs' physical condition?

3. **R:** What does Hal claim is the reason the dogs are unable to move the sled?

4. **I:** What is the probable reason that Buck runs the sled wildly down the street of Skaguay?

5. **R:** Why shouldn't fourteen dogs drag one sled?

6. **I:** What actions on the part of Charles and Hal justify the lack of confidence Buck feels toward them?

7. **R:** What warning does John Thornton give to Hal about the ice?

8. **I:** What actions on the part of John Thornton show his courage and compassion?

Synthesizing

9. What causes inexperienced people like Charles, Hal, and Mercedes to "adventure the North"? What sort of image do they have of the North? How is that image different from the reality?

10. What kind of people does Thornton recognize Charles, Hal, and Mercedes to be? Does Thornton have respect for them? Why, or why not?

Understanding Literature (QUESTIONS FOR DISCUSSION)

1. Conflict. A **conflict** is a struggle between two forces in a literary work. A character may struggle against another character, against the forces of nature, against society or social norms, against fate, or against some element within himself or herself. A struggle that takes place between a character and some outside force is called an **external conflict.** A struggle that takes place within a character is called an **internal conflict.** At the end of this chapter, the character John Thornton experiences both kinds of conflict—external and internal. Against what external conflict does Thornton struggle? What internal conflict causes Thornton to hesitate before defending Buck from Hal?

2. Character. A **character** is a person (or sometimes an animal) who figures in the action of a literary work. Two types of characters include a **one-dimensional character** and a **three-dimensional character.** Hal, Charles, and Mercedes are examples of one-dimensional characters— characters who exhibit a single dominant quality or character trait. What dominant quality or trait does each of these characters exhibit? John Thornton is an example of a three-dimensional character—a character who exhibits the complexity of traits associated with actual human beings. What traits does Thornton exhibit at the end of this chapter?

CHAPTER VI

For the Love of a Man

When John Thornton froze his feet in the previous December, his partners had made him comfortable and left him to get well, going on themselves up the river to get out a raft of saw-logs for Dawson. He was still limping slightly at the time he rescued Buck, but with the continued warm weather even the slight limp left him. And here, lying by the river bank through the long spring days, watching the running water, listening lazily to the songs of birds and the hum of nature, Buck slowly won back his strength.

A rest comes very good after one has traveled three thousand miles, and it must be confessed that Buck waxed lazy as his wounds healed, his muscles swelled out, and the flesh came back to cover his bones. For that matter, they were all loafing, Buck, John Thornton—and Skeet and Nig—waiting for the raft to come that was to carry them down to Dawson. Skeet was a little Irish setter who early made friends with Buck, who, in a dying condition, was unable to resent her first advances. She had the doctor trait which some dogs possess; and as a mother cat washes her kittens, so she washed and cleansed Buck's wounds. Regularly, each morning after he had finished his breakfast, she performed her self-appointed task, till he came to look for her <u>ministrations</u> as much as he did for Thornton's. Nig, equally friendly, though less demonstrative, was a huge black dog, half-bloodhound

◀ Why is Skeet able to become friends with Buck?

| Words For Everyday Use | **min • is • tra • tion** (min´is trā´shən) *n.*, act of giving care, help, or service |

and half-deerhound, with eyes that laughed and a boundless good nature.

► What surprises Buck about these dogs? What past experience causes this surprise?

To Buck's surprise these dogs manifested no jealousy toward him. They seemed to share the kindliness and largeness of John Thornton. As Buck grew stronger they enticed him into all sorts of ridiculous games, in which Thornton himself could not forebear to join; and in this fashion Buck romped through his <u>convalescence</u> and into a new existence. Love, genuine passionate love, was his for the first time. This he had never experienced at Judge Miller's down in the sun-kissed Santa Clara Valley. With the Judge's sons, hunting and tramping, it had been a working partnership; with the Judge's grandsons, a sort of pompous guardianship; and with the Judge himself, a stately and dignified friendship. But love that was feverish and burning, that was adoration, that was madness, it had taken John Thornton to arouse.

► What were Buck's relationships with other masters like? What makes John Thornton special?

This man had saved his life, which was something; but, further, he was the ideal master. Other men saw to the welfare of their dogs from a sense of duty and business expediency; he saw to the welfare of his as if they were his own children, because he could not help it. And he saw further. He never forgot a kindly greeting or a cheering word, and to sit down for a long talk with them ("gas" he called it) was as much his delight as theirs. He had a way of taking Buck's head roughly between his hands, and resting his own head upon Buck's, of shaking him back and forth, the while calling him ill names that to Buck were love names. Buck knew no greater joy than that rough embrace and the sound of murmured oaths, and at each jerk back and forth it seemed that his heart would be shaken out of his body so great

► In what manner does Thornton see to the welfare of his dogs? In what does he delight?

Words
For
Everyday
Use

con • va • les • cence (kän´və ləs' əns) n., gradual recovery after illness or injury

was its ecstasy. And when, released, he sprang to his feet, his mouth laughing, his eyes eloquent, his throat vibrant with unuttered sound, and in that fashion remained without movement, John Thornton would reverently exclaim, "God! you can all but speak!"

Buck had a trick of love expression that was akin to hurt. He would often seize Thornton's hand in his mouth and close so fiercely that the flesh bore the impress of his teeth for some time afterward. And as Buck understood the oaths to be love words, so the man understood this feigned bite for a caress.

For the most part, however, Buck's love was expressed in adoration. While he went wild with happiness when Thornton touched him or spoke to him, he did not seek these tokens. Unlike Skeet, who was wont to shove her nose under Thornton's hand and nudge and nudge till petted, or Nig, who would stalk up and rest his great head on Thornton's knee, Buck was content to adore at a distance. He would lie by the hour, eager, alert, at Thornton's feet, looking up into his face, dwelling upon it, studying it, following with keenest interest each fleeting expression, every movement or change of feature. Or, as chance might have it, he would lie farther away, to the side or rear, watching the outlines of the man and the occasional movements of his body. And often, such was the communion in which they lived, the strength of Buck's gaze would draw John Thornton's head around, and he would return the gaze, without speech, his heart shining out of his eyes as Buck's heart shone out.

For a long time after his rescue, Buck did not like Thornton to get out of his sight. From the moment he left the tent to when he entered it again, Buck would follow at his heels. His <u>transient</u> masters since

◀ *Why does Buck not like to lose sight of Thornton?*

he had come into the Northland had bred in him a fear that no master could be permanent. He was afraid that Thornton would pass out of his life as Perrault and François and the Scot had passed out. Even in the night, in his dreams, he was haunted by this fear. At such times he would shake off sleep and creep through the chill to the flap of the tent, where he would stand and listen to the sound of his master's breathing.

► What two forces are active in Buck? Which is stronger?

But in spite of this great love he bore John Thornton, which seemed to bespeak the soft civilizing influence, the strain of the primitive, which the Northland had aroused in him, remained alive and active. Faithfulness and devotion, things born of fire and roof, were his; yet he retained his wildness and wiliness. He was a thing of the wild, come in from the wild to sit by John Thornton's fire, rather than a dog of the soft Southland stamped with the marks of generations of civilization. Because of his very great love, he could not steal from this man, but from any other man, in any other camp, he did not hesitate an instant; while the cunning with which he stole enabled him to escape detection.

His face and body were scored by the teeth of many dogs, and he fought as fiercely as ever and more shrewdly. Skeet and Nig were too good-natured for quarreling—besides, they belonged to John Thornton; but the strange dog, no matter what the breed or valor, swiftly acknowledged Buck's supremacy or found himself struggling for life with a terrible antagonist. And Buck was merciless. He had learned well the law of club and fang, and he never forewent an advantage or drew back from a foe he had started on the way to death. He had lessoned from Spitz, and from the chief fighting dogs of the police and mail, and knew there was no middle course. He must master or be mastered; while to show mercy was a weakness. Mercy did not exist in the primordial life. It was misunderstood for fear, and such misunderstandings

► What emotion does not exist in the "primordial life"? Why doesn't this emotion exist?

made for death. Kill or be killed, eat or be eaten, was the law; and this <u>mandate</u>, down out of the depths of Time, he obeyed.

He was older than the days he had seen and the breaths he had drawn. He linked the past with the present, and the eternity behind him throbbed through him in a mighty rhythm to which he swayed as the tides and seasons swayed. He sat by John Thornton's fire, a broad-breasted dog, white-fanged and long-furred; but behind him were the shades of all manner of dogs, half-wolves and wild wolves, urgent and prompting, tasting the savor of the meat he ate, thirsting for the water he drank, scenting the wind with him, listening with him and telling him the sounds made by the wildlife in the forest, dictating his moods, directing his actions, lying down to sleep with him when he lay down, and dreaming with him and beyond him and becoming themselves the stuff of his dreams.

◀ *In what way is Buck affected by links to the past?*

So <u>peremptorily</u> did these shades beckon him, that each day mankind and the claims of mankind slipped farther from him. Deep in the forest a call was sounding, and as often as he heard this call mysteriously thrilling and luring, he felt compelled to turn his back upon the fire and the beaten earth around it, and to plunge into the forest, and on and on, he knew not where or why; nor did he wonder where or why, the call sounding imperiously, deep in the forest. But as often as he gained the soft unbroken earth and the green shade, the love for John Thornton drew him back to the fire again.

◀ *What compels Buck to plunge into the forest? What compels him to come back to the fire?*

Thornton alone held him. The rest of mankind was as nothing. Chance travelers might praise or pet him; but he was cold under it all, and from a too demonstrative man he would get up and walk away.

Words
For
Everyday
Use

man • date (man'dāt˘) *n.,* command

per • emp • to • ri • ly (pər emp'tə rə lē) *adv.,* finally; absolutely

► What is Buck's attitude toward Hans and Pete? How do Hans and Pete treat Buck?

When Thornton's partners, Hans and Pete, arrived on the long-expected raft, Buck refused to notice them till he learned they were close to Thornton; after that he tolerated them in a passive sort of way, accepting favors from them as though he favored them by accepting. They were of the same large type as Thornton, living close to the earth, thinking simply and seeing clearly; and ere they swung the raft into the big eddy by the sawmill at Dawson, they understood Buck and his ways, and did not insist upon an intimacy such as obtained with Skeet and Nig.

For Thornton, however, his love seemed to grow and grow. He, alone among men, could put a pack upon Buck's back in the summer traveling. Nothing was too great for Buck to do, when Thornton commanded. One day (they had grubstaked[1] themselves from the proceeds of the raft and left Dawson for the headwaters of the Tanana) the men and dogs were sitting on the crest of a cliff which fell away, straight down, to naked bedrock three hundred feet below. John Thornton was sitting near the edge, Buck at his shoulder. A thoughtless whim seized Thornton, and

► What experiment does Thornton try on a whim? What does it prove?

he drew the attention of Hans and Pete to the experiment he had in mind. "Jump, Buck!" he commanded, sweeping his arm out and over the chasm. The next instant he was grappling with Buck on the extreme edge, while Hans and Pete were dragging them back into safety.

"It's uncanny," Pete said, after it was over and they had caught their speech.

Thornton shook his head. "No, it is splendid, and it is terrible, too. Do you know, it sometimes makes me afraid."

"I'm not hankering to be the man that lays hands on you while he's around," Pete announced conclusively, nodding his head toward Buck.

---

1. **grubstaked.** Set themselves up with money and supplies

"Py Jingo!" was Hans's contribution. "Not mine-self either."

It was at Circle City, ere the year was out, that Pete's apprehensions were realized. "Black" Burton, a man evil-tempered and <u>malicious</u>, had been pick-ing a quarrel with a tenderfoot² at the bar, when Thornton stepped good-naturedly between. Buck, as was his custom, was lying in a corner, head on paws, watching his master's every action. Burton struck out, without warning, straight from the shoulder. Thornton was sent spinning, and saved himself from falling only by clutching the rail of the bar. Those who were looking on heard what was nei-ther bark nor yelp, but a something which is best described as a roar, and they saw Buck's body rise up in the air as he left the floor for Burton's throat. The man saved his life by instinctively throwing out his arm, but was hurled backward to the floor with Buck on top of him. Buck loosed his teeth from the flesh of the arm and drove in again for the throat. This time the man succeeded only in partly blocking, and his throat was torn open. Then the crowd was upon Buck, and he was driven off; but while a surgeon checked the bleeding, he prowled up and down, growling furiously, attempting to rush in, and being forced back by an array of hostile clubs. A "miners' meeting," called on the spot, decided that the dog had sufficient <u>provocation</u>, and Buck was dis-charged. But his reputation was made, and from that day his name spread through every camp in Alaska.

◄ *What reputation does Buck gain?*

Later on, in the fall of the year, he saved John Thornton's life in quite another fashion. The three partners were lining a long and narrow poling-boat

---

2. **tenderfoot.** Any newcomer, novice, or beginner

Words For Everyday Use

ma • li • cious (mə lish´əs) *adj.*, intentionally spiteful; harmful

prov • o • ca • tion (präv´ə kā´shən) *n.*, something that stirs up feelings or action, especially a cause of resentment or irritation

down a bad stretch of rapids on the Forty Mile Creek. Hans and Pete moved along the bank, snubbing[3] with a thin Manila rope[4] from tree to tree, while Thornton remained in the boat, helping its descent by means of a pole, and shouting directions to the shore. Buck, on the bank, worried and anxious, kept abreast of the boat, his eyes never off his master.

At a particularly bad spot, where a ledge of barely submerged rocks jutted out into the river, Hans cast off the rope, and, while Thornton poled the boat out into the stream, ran down the bank with the end in his hand to snub the boat when it had cleared the ledge. This it did, and was flying downstream in a current as swift as a millrace,[5] when Hans checked it with the rope and checked too suddenly. The boat flirted over and snubbed in to the bank bottom up, while Thornton, flung sheer out of it, was carried downstream toward the worst part of the rapids, a stretch of wild water in which no swimmer could live.

► What does Buck do to save Thornton's life? What makes progress difficult? What danger lies ahead?

Buck had sprung in on the instant; and at the end of three hundred yards, amid a mad swirl of water, he overhauled Thornton. When he felt him grasp his tail, Buck headed for the bank, swimming with all his splendid strength. But the progress shoreward was slow, the progress downstream amazingly rapid. From below came the fatal roaring where the wild current went wilder and was rent in shreds and spray by the rocks which thrust through like the teeth of an enormous comb. The suck of the water as it took the beginning of the last steep pitch was frightful,

---

3. **snubbing.** Moving a boat by turning it around a post
4. **Manila rope.** Strong rope made of hemp from Manila, capital of the Philippines
5. **millrace.** Current of water that drives a mill wheel

Words For Everyday Use

sub • merged (sub mɐrjd´) *adj.*, covered by water

and Thornton knew that the shore was impossible. He scraped furiously over a rock, bruised across a second, and struck a third with crushing force. He clutched its slippery top with both hands, releasing Buck, and above the roar of the churning water shouted: "Go, Buck! Go!"

Buck could not hold his own, and swept on downstream, struggling desperately, but unable to win back. When he heard Thornton's command repeated, he partly reared out of the water, throwing his head high, as though for a last look, then turned obediently toward the bank. He swam powerfully and was dragged ashore by Pete and Hans at the very point where swimming ceased to be possible and destruction began.

They knew that the time a man could cling to a slippery rock in the face of that driving current was a matter of minutes, and they ran as fast as they could up the bank to a point far above where Thornton was hanging on. They attached the line with which they had been snubbing the boat to Buck's neck and shoulders, being careful that it should neither strangle him nor impede his swimming, and launched him into the stream. He struck out boldly, but not straight enough into the stream. He discovered the mistake too late, when Thornton was abreast of him and a bare half-dozen strokes away while he was being carried helplessly past.

◀ *What mistake does Buck make? What should he have done?*

Hans promptly snubbed with the rope, as though Buck were a boat. The rope thus tightening on him in the sweep of the current, he was jerked under the surface, and under the surface he remained till his body struck against the bank and he was hauled out. He was half-drowned, and Hans and Pete threw themselves upon him, pounding the breath into him and the water out of him. He staggered to his feet and fell down. The faint sound of Thornton's voice came to them, and though they could not

► *What spurs Buck on to further action?*

make out the words of it, they knew that he was in his extremity. His master's voice acted on Buck like an electric shock. He sprang to his feet and ran up the bank ahead of the men to the point of his previous departure.

Again the rope was attached and he was launched, and again he struck out, but this time straight into the stream. He had miscalculated once, but he would not be guilty of it a second time. Hans paid out the rope, permitting no slack, while Pete kept it clear of coils. Buck held on till he was on a line straight above Thornton; then he turned, and with the speed of an express train headed down upon him. Thornton saw him coming, and, as Buck struck him like a battering ram, with the whole force of the current behind him, he reached up and closed with both arms around the shaggy neck. Hans snubbed the rope around the tree, and Buck and Thornton were jerked under the water. Strangling, suffocating, sometimes one uppermost and sometimes the other, dragging over the jagged bottom, smashing against rocks and snags, they veered in to the bank.

Thornton came to, belly downward and being violently propelled back and forth across a drift log by Hans and Pete. His first glance was for Buck, over whose limp and apparently lifeless body Nig was setting up a howl, while Skeet was licking the wet face and closed eyes. Thornton was himself bruised and battered, and he went carefully over Buck's body, when he had been brought around, finding three broken ribs.

"That settles it," he announced. "We camp right here." And camp they did, till Buck's ribs knitted and he was able to travel.

Words For Everyday Use

ex • trem • i • ty (ek strem´ ə tē) *n.*, state of extreme necessity or danger

That winter, at Dawson, Buck performed another exploit, not so heroic, perhaps, but one that put his name many notches higher on the totem-pole[6] of Alaskan fame. This exploit was particularly gratifying to the three men; for they stood in need of the outfit which it furnished, and were enabled to make a long-desired trip into the virgin East, where miners had not yet appeared. It was brought about by a conversation in the Eldorado Saloon, in which men waxed boastful of their favorite dogs. Buck, because of his record, was the target for these men, and Thornton was driven stoutly to defend him. At the end of half an hour one man stated that his dog could start a sled with five hundred pounds and walk off with it; a second bragged six hundred for his dog; and a third, seven hundred.

◀ What effect does Buck's next act have for him? for Thornton and his friends?

"Pooh! pooh!" said John Thornton; "Buck can start a thousand pounds."

◀ What boast does Thornton make? What happens as a result of this boast?

"And break it out? and walk off with it for a hundred yards?" demanded Matthewson, a Bonanza King, he of the seven-hundred <u>vaunt</u>.

"And break it out, and walk off with it for a hundred yards," John Thornton said coolly.

"Well," Matthewson said, slowly and deliberately, so that all could hear, "I've got a thousand dollars that says he can't. And there it is." So saying, he slammed a sack of gold dust of the size of a bologna sausage down upon the bar.

Nobody spoke. Thornton's bluff, if bluff it was, had been called. He could feel a flush of warm blood creeping up his face. His tongue had tricked him. He

---

6. **totem-pole.** Pole or post carved and painted with totems, or images of animals or natural objects believed to be related to a family's heritage, often erected in front of their dwellings by Native Americans from the northwest coast of North America

Words For Everyday Use

vaunt (vônt) *n.,* boast or brag

► Does Thornton believe Buck can start a thousand pounds? Does he regret his statement?

did not know whether Buck could start a thousand pounds. Half a ton! The enormousness of it appalled him. He had great faith in Buck's strength and had often thought him capable of starting such a load; but never, as now, had he faced the possibility of it, the eyes of a dozen men fixed upon him, silent and waiting. Further, he had no thousand dollars; nor had Hans or Pete.

"I've got a sled standing outside now, with twenty fifty-pound sacks of flour on it," Matthewson went on with brutal directness; "so don't let that hinder you."

Thornton did not reply. He did not know what to say. He glanced from face to face in the absent way of a man who has lost the power of thought and is seeking somewhere to find the thing that will start it going again. The face of Jim O'Brien, a Mastodon King and old-time comrade, caught his eyes. It was as a cue to him, seeming to rouse him to do what he would never have dreamed of doing.

► What rouses Thornton to action? What does he ask O'Brien? Does O'Brien believe Buck can do it?

"Can you lend me a thousand?" he asked, almost in a whisper.

"Sure," answered O'Brien, thumping down a plethoric sack by the side of Matthewson's. "Though it's little faith I'm having, John, that the beast can do the trick."

The Eldorado emptied its occupants into the street to see the test. The tables were deserted, and the dealers and gamekeepers came forth to see the outcome of the wager and to lay odds. Several hundred men, furred and mittened, banked around the sled within easy distance. Matthewson's sled, loaded with a thousand pounds of flour, had been standing for a couple of hours, and in the intense cold (it was sixty below zero) the runners had frozen fast to the

Words For Everyday Use	**ple • thor • ic** (plə thôr´ik) adj., characterized by excess or profusion

hard-packed snow. Men offered odds of two to one that Buck could not budge the sled. A quibble arose concerning the phrase "break out." O'Brien contended it was Thornton's privilege to knock the runners loose, leaving Buck to "break it out" from a dead standstill. Matthewson insisted that the phrase included breaking the runners from the frozen grip of the snow. A majority of the men who had witnessed the making of the bet decided in his favor, whereat the odds went up to three to one against Buck.

There were no takers. Not a man believed him capable of the feat. Thornton had been hurried into the wager, heavy with doubt; and now that he looked at the sled itself, the concrete fact, with the regular team of ten dogs curled up in the snow before it, the more impossible the task appeared. Matthewson waxed jubilant.

"Three to one!" he proclaimed. "I'll lay you another thousand at that figure, Thornton. What d'ye say?"

Thornton's doubt was strong in his face, but his fighting spirit was aroused—the fighting spirit that soars above odds, fails to recognize the impossible, and is deaf to all save the clamor for battle. He called Hans and Pete to him. Their sacks were slim, and with his own the three partners could rake together only two hundred dollars. In the ebb of their fortunes, this sum was their total capital; yet they laid it unhesitatingly against Matthewson's six hundred.

The team of ten dogs was unhitched, and Buck, with his own harness, was put into the sled. He had caught the <u>contagion</u> of the excitement, and he felt that in some way he must do a great thing for John Thornton. Murmurs of admiration at his splendid

◄ *What does Buck sense?*

Words For Everyday Use	**con • ta • gion** (kən tā′jən) *n.*, spreading of an emotion, idea, or custom from person to person until many are affected

appearance went up. He was in perfect condition, without an ounce of superfluous flesh, and the one hundred and fifty pounds that he weighed were so many pounds of grit and <u>virility</u>. His furry coat shone with the sheen of silk. Down the neck and across the shoulders, his mane, in repose as it was, half bristled and seemed to lift with every movement, as though excess of vigor made each particular hair alive and active. The great breast and heavy forelegs were no more than in proportion with the rest of the body, where the muscles showed in tight rolls underneath the skin. Men felt these muscles and proclaimed them hard as iron, and the odds went down to two to one.

"Gad, sir! Gad, sir!" stuttered a member of the latest dynasty, a king of the Skookum Benches. "I offer you eight hundred for him, sir, before the test, sir; eight hundred just as he stands."

Thornton shook his head and stepped to Buck's side.

"You must stand off from him," Matthewson protested. "Free play and plenty of room."

The crowd fell silent; only could be heard the voices of the gamblers vainly offering two to one. Everybody acknowledged Buck a magnificent animal, but twenty fifty-pound sacks of flour bulked too large in their eyes for them to loosen their pouch-strings.

Thornton knelt down by Buck's side. He took his head in his two hands and rested cheek on cheek. He did not playfully shake him, as was his wont, or murmur soft love curses; but he whispered in his ear. "As you love me, Buck. As you love me," was what he whispered. Buck whined with suppressed eagerness.

▶ *What does Thornton whisper to Buck?*

The crowd was watching curiously. The affair was growing mysterious. It seemed like a conjuration. As Thornton got to his feet, Buck seized his mittened hand between his jaws, pressing in with his teeth and releasing slowly, half-reluctantly. It was the answer, in terms, not of speech, but of love. Thornton stepped well back.

"Now, Buck," he said.

Buck tightened the traces, then slacked them for a matter of several inches. It was the way he had learned.

"Gee!" Thornton's voice rang out, sharp in the tense silence.

Buck swung to the right, ending the movement in a plunge that took up the slack and with a sudden jerk arrested his one hundred and fifty pounds. The load quivered, and from under the runners arose a crisp crackling.

"Haw!" Thornton commanded.

Buck duplicated the maneuver, this time to the left. The crackling turned into a snapping, the sled pivoting and the runners slipping and grating several inches to the side. The sled was broken out. Men were holding their breaths, intensely unconscious of the fact.

"Now, MUSH!"

Thornton's command cracked out like a pistol shot. Buck threw himself forward, tightening the traces with a jarring lunge. His whole body was gathered compactly together in the tremendous effort, the muscles writhing and knotting like live things under the silky fur. His great chest was low to the ground, his head forward and down, while his feet were flying like mad, the claws scarring the hard-packed snow in parallel grooves. The sled swayed and trembled, half-started forward. One of his feet slipped, and one man groaned aloud. Then the sled lurched ahead in what appeared a rapid succession of jerks, though it never really came to a dead stop again . . . half an inch . . . an inch . . . two inches. . . . The jerks perceptibly diminished; as the sled gained momentum, he caught them up, till it was moving steadily along.

▶ What shows that the growing tension has been released?

Men gasped and began to breathe again, unaware that for a moment they had ceased to breathe. Thornton was running behind, encouraging Buck with short, cheery words. The distance had been measured off, and as he neared the pile of firewood which marked the end of the hundred yards, a cheer began to grow and grow, which burst into a roar as he passed the firewood and halted at command. Every man was tearing himself loose, even Matthewson. Hats and mittens were flying in the air. Men were shaking hands, it did not matter with whom, and bubbling over in a general incoherent babel.

▶ How does the crowd react to Buck's success?

But Thornton fell on his knees beside Buck. Head was against head, and he was shaking him back and forth. Those who hurried up heard him cursing Buck, and he cursed him long and fervently, and softly and lovingly.

"Gad, sir! Gad, sir!" spluttered the Skookum Bench King. "I'll give you a thousand for him, sir, a thousand, sir—twelve hundred, sir."

Thornton rose to his feet. His eyes were wet. The tears were streaming frankly down his cheeks. "Sir," he said to the Skookum Bench King, "no, sir. You can go to hell, sir. It's the best I can do for you, sir."

Buck seized Thornton's hand in his teeth. Thornton shook him back and forth. As though animated by a common impulse, the onlookers drew back to a respectful distance; nor were they again indiscreet enough to interrupt.

| Words For Everyday Use | in • co • her • ent (in´kō hir´ ənt) *adj.*, not logically connected; disjointed; rambling |
| | ba • bel (bā´ bəl) *n.*, confusion of voices, languages, or sounds |

Responding to the Selection

Which of Buck's actions for Thornton do you find most admirable? Which escapade is most exciting? Discuss your opinions and why you feel this way with two or three of your classmates.

Reviewing the Selection

Recalling and Interpreting

1. **R:** What kind of master is John Thornton to Buck?

2. **I:** What actions on the part of John Thornton show his particular affection for Buck?

3. **R:** What command does Thornton give to Buck on the crest of the cliff?

4. **I:** What is probably the reason that Thornton gives the command?

5. **R:** What heroic feat does Buck perform on the rapids of Forty-Mile Creek?

6. **I:** What value does Thornton show that he places on Buck when he says "That settles it. We camp right here"? What do you think about Thornton giving the command?

7. **R:** What feat does Matthewson bet Thornton that Buck cannot do?

8. **I:** What action on the part of Buck secures his place "on the totem-pole of Alaskan fame"?

Synthesizing

9. What is the difference between the feelings that Buck has toward John Thornton and his feelings toward his other masters, such as Judge Miller and François and Perrault?

10. What qualities does John Thornton possess that allow him to be the only hold humankind has on Buck?

Understanding Literature (QUESTIONS FOR DISCUSSION)

Characterization. Characterization is the use of literary techniques to create a character. Two of these techniques, direct description and portrayal of a character's behavior, are used in the following passage from this chapter: "He sat by John Thornton's fire, a broad-breasted dog, white-fanged and long-furred; but behind him were the shades of all manner of dogs, half-wolves and wild wolves, urgent and prompting, tasting the savor of the meat he ate, thirsting for the water he drank, scenting the wind with him, listening with him and telling him the sounds made by the wildlife in the forest, dictating his moods, directing his actions, lying down to sleep with him when he lay down, and dreaming with him and beyond him and becoming themselves the stuff of his dreams." What aspects of Buck's character are revealed by the description of him sitting by the fire? How does this contrast with the characterization of "the shades of all manner of dogs"? Who are they? What kind of influence or power do they have upon the character of Buck?

CHAPTER VII

The Sounding of the Call

When Buck earned sixteen hundred dollars in five minutes for John Thornton, he made it possible for his master to pay off certain debts and to journey with his partners into the East after a fabled lost mine, the history of which was as old as the history of the country. Many men had sought it; few had found it; and more than a few there were who had never returned from the quest. This lost mine was steeped in tragedy and shrouded in mystery. No one knew of the first man. The oldest tradition stopped before it got back to him. From the beginning there had been an ancient and ramshackle cabin. Dying men had sworn to it, and to the mine the site of which it marked, clinching their testimony with nuggets that were unlike any known grade of gold in the Northland.

◀ What did Buck's victory enable John Thornton to do?

But no living man had looted this treasure house, and the dead were dead; wherefore John Thornton and Pete and Hans, with Buck and half a dozen other dogs, faced into the East on an unknown trail to achieve where men and dogs as good as themselves had failed. They sledded seventy miles up the Yukon, swung to the left into the Stewart River, passed the Mayo and the McQuestion, and held on until the Stewart itself became a streamlet, threading the upstanding peaks, which marked the backbone of the continent.

John Thornton asked little of man or nature. He was unafraid of the wild. With a handful of salt and a rifle he could plunge into the wilderness and fare wherever he pleased and as long as he pleased. Being in no haste, Indian fashion, he hunted his dinner in the course of the day's travel; and if he failed to find it, like the Indian, he kept on traveling, secure in the

THE SOUNDING OF THE CALL **99**

knowledge that sooner or later he would come to it. So, on this great journey into the East, straight meat was the bill of fare[1], ammunition and tools principally made up the load on the sled, and the timecard was drawn upon the limitless future.

▶ How does Buck feel about this adventure? What does he enjoy about it?

To Buck it was boundless delight, this hunting, fishing, and indefinite wandering through strange places. For weeks at a time they would hold on steadily, day after day; and for weeks upon end they would camp, here and there, the dogs loafing and the men burning holes through frozen muck and gravel and washing countless pans of dirt by the heat of the fire. Sometimes they went hungry, sometimes they feasted riotously, all according to the abundance of game and the fortune of hunting. Summer arrived, and dogs and men packed on their backs, rafted across blue mountain lakes, and descended or ascended unknown rivers in slender boats whipsawed[2] from the standing forest.

The months came and went, and back and forth they twisted through the uncharted vastness, where no men were and yet where men had been if the Lost Cabin were true. They went across divides in summer blizzards, shivered under the midnight sun on naked mountains between the timber line and the eternal snows, dropped into summer valleys amid swarming gnats and flies, and in the shadows of glaciers picked strawberries and flowers as ripe and fair as any the Southland could boast. In the fall of the year they penetrated a weird lake country, sad and silent, where wildfowl had been, but where then there was no life nor sign of life—only the blowing of chill winds, the forming of ice in sheltered places, and the melancholy rippling of waves on lonely beaches.

---

1. **bill of fare.** Menu
2. **whipsawed.** Cut with a whipsaw, a two-handled crosscut saw, five-and-a-half to seven feet long

And through another winter they wandered on the <u>obliterated</u> trails of men who had gone before. Once, they came upon a path blazed through the forest, an ancient path, and the Lost Cabin seemed very near. But the path began nowhere and ended nowhere, and it remained mystery, as the man who made it and the reason he made it remained mystery. Another time they chanced upon the time-graven wreckage of a hunting lodge, and amid the shreds of rotted blankets John Thornton found a long-barreled flintlock.[3] He knew it for a Hudson Bay Company gun of the young days in the Northwest, when such a gun was worth its height in beaver skins packed flat. And that was all—no hint as to the man who in an early day had reared the lodge and left the gun among the blankets.

Spring came on once more, and at the end of all their wandering they found, not the Lost Cabin, but a shallow placer[4] in a broad valley where the gold showed like yellow butter across the bottom of the washingpan. They sought no farther. Each day they worked earned them thousands of dollars in clean dust and nuggets, and they worked every day. The gold was sacked in moosehide bags, fifty pounds to the bag, and piled like so much firewood outside the spruce-bough lodge. Like giants they toiled, days flashing on the heels of days like dreams as they heaped the treasure up.

There was nothing for the dogs to do, save the hauling in of meat now and again that Thornton killed, and Buck spent long hours musing by the fire. The vision of the short-legged hairy man came to

---

3. **flintlock.** Gun with a lock in which a flint in the hammer strikes a metal plate to produce a spark that ignites the powder
4. **placer.** Gravel or sand containing ore

Words For Everyday Use	ob • lit • er • at • ed (ō blit´ər āt əd) *part.,* erased; destroyed

him more frequently, now that there was little work to be done; and often, blinking by the fire, Buck wandered with him in that other world which he remembered.

► What does the hairy man feel most often?

The salient thing of this other world seemed fear. When he watched the hairy man sleeping by the fire, head between his knees and hands clasped above, Buck saw that he slept restlessly, with many starts and awakenings, at which times he would peer fearfully into the darkness and fling more wood upon the fire. Did they walk by the beach of a sea, where the hairy man gathered shellfish and ate them as he gathered, it was with eyes that roved everywhere for hidden danger and with legs prepared to run like the wind at its first appearance. Through the forest they crept noiselessly, Buck at the hairy man's heels; and they were alert and vigilant, the pair of them, ears twitching and moving and nostrils quivering, for the man heard and smelled as keenly as Buck. The hairy man could spring up into the trees and travel ahead as fast as on the ground, swinging by the arms from limb to limb, sometimes a dozen feet apart, letting go and catching, never falling, never missing his grip. In fact, he seemed as much at home among the trees as on the ground; and Buck had memories of nights of <u>vigil</u> spent beneath trees wherein the hairy man roosted, holding on tightly as he slept.

And closely akin to the visions of the hairy man was the call still sounding in the depths of the forest. It filled him with a great unrest and strange desires. It caused him to feel a vague, sweet gladness, and he was aware of wild yearnings and stirrings for he knew not what. Sometimes he pursued the call into the forest, looking for it as though it were a <u>tangible</u> thing,

| Words For Everyday Use | vig • il (vij´əl) *n.*, watch kept during normal sleeping hours |
| | tan • gi • ble (tan´jə bəl) *adj.*, touchable |

barking softly or defiantly, as the mood might dictate. He would thrust his nose into the cool wood moss, or into the black soil where long grasses grew, and snort with joy at the fat earth smells; or he would crouch for hours, as if in concealment, behind fungus-covered trunks of fallen trees, wide-eyed and wide-eared to all that moved and sounded about him. It might be, lying thus, that he hoped to surprise this call he could not understand. But he did not know why he did these various things. He was impelled to do them, and did not reason about them at all.

Irresistible impulses seized him. He would be lying in camp, dozing lazily in the heat of the day, when suddenly his head would lift and his ears cock up, intent and listening, and he would spring to his feet and dash away, and on and on, for hours, through the forest aisles and across the open spaces. He loved to run down dry watercourses, and to creep and spy upon the bird life in the woods. For a day at a time he would lie in the underbrush where he could watch the partridges drumming and strutting up and down. But especially he loved to run in the dim twilight of the summer midnights, listening to the subdued and sleepy murmurs of the forest, reading signs and sounds as man may read a book, and seeking for the mysterious something that called—called, waking or sleeping, at all times, for him to come.

One night he sprang from sleep with a start, eager-eyed, nostrils quivering and scenting, his mane bristling in <u>recurrent</u> waves. From the forest came the call (or one note of it, for the call was many noted), distinct and definite as never before—a long-drawn howl, like, yet unlike, any noise made

◄ *What wakes Buck? Why is he attracted to it?*

Words For Everyday Use

re • cur • rent (ri kʉr´ənt) *adj.*, occurring or appearing again

by a husky dog. And he knew it, in the old familiar way, as a sound heard before. He sprang through the sleeping camp and in swift silence dashed through the woods. As he drew closer to the cry he went more slowly, with caution in every movement, till he came to an open place among the trees, and looking out saw, erect on haunches, with nose pointed to the sky, a long, lean, timber wolf.

He had made no noise, yet it ceased from its howling and tried to sense his presence. Buck stalked into the open, half crouching, body gathered compactly together, tail straight and stiff, feet falling with unwonted care. Every movement advertised <u>commingled</u> threatening and overture of friendliness. It was the menacing truce that marks the meeting of wild beasts that prey. But the wolf fled at sight of him. He followed, with wild leapings, in a frenzy to overtake. He ran him into a blind channel, in the bed of the creek, where a timber jam barred the way. The wolf whirled about, pivoting on his hind legs after the fashion of Joe and of all cornered husky dogs, snarling and bristling, clipping his teeth together in a continuous and rapid succession of snaps.

► How does Buck treat the wolf? How does the wolf respond?

Buck did not attack, but circled him about and hedged him in with friendly advances. The wolf was suspicious and afraid; for Buck made three of him in weight, while his head barely reached Buck's shoulder. Watching his chance he darted away, and the chase was resumed. Time and again he was cornered, and the thing repeated, though he was in poor condition or Buck could not so easily have overtaken him. He would run till Buck's head was even with his flank, when he would whirl around at bay, only to dash away again at the first opportunity.

Words For Everyday Use	com • min • gled (kəm miŋ´ gəld) adj., intermixed

But in the end Buck's <u>pertinacity</u> was rewarded; for the wolf, finding that no harm was intended, finally sniffed noses with him. Then they became friendly, and played about in the nervous, half-coy way with which fierce beasts <u>belie</u> their fierceness. After some time of this the wolf started off at an easy <u>lope</u> in a manner that plainly showed he was going somewhere. He made it clear to Buck that he was to come, and they ran side by side through the <u>somber</u> twilight, straight up the creek bed, into the gorge from which it issued, and across the bleak divide where it took its rise.

On the opposite slope of the watershed they came down into a level country where were great stretches of forest and many streams, and through these great stretches they ran steadily, hour after hour, the sun rising higher and the day growing warmer. Buck was wildly glad. He knew he was at last answering the call, running by the side of his wood brother toward the place from where the call surely came. Old memories were coming upon him fast, and he was stirring to them as of old he stirred to the realities of which they were the shadows. He had done this thing before, somewhere in that other and dimly remembered world, and he was doing it again, now, running free in the open, the unpacked earth underfoot, the wide sky overhead.

◀ *What does Buck believe is happening? How does he feel about this?*

They stopped by a running stream to drink, and, stopping, Buck remembered John Thornton. He sat down. The wolf started on toward the place from where the call surely came, then returned to him, sniffing noses and making actions as though to encourage him. But Buck turned about and started slowly on the back track. For the better part of an hour the wild brother ran by his side, whining softly.

◀ *What does Buck remember?*

Words For Everyday Use

per • ti • nac • i • ty (pᵾr´tə nãs´ə tē) n., stubborn persistance, obstinacy

be • lie (bē lī) vt., disguise, misrepresent

lope (lōp) n., long, easy stride

som • ber (säm´bər) adj., dark, dull

Then he sat down, pointed his nose upward, and howled. It was a mournful howl, and as Buck held steadily on his way he heard it grow faint and fainter until it was lost in the distance.

John Thornton was eating dinner when Buck dashed into camp and sprang upon him in a frenzy of affection, overturning him, scrambling upon him, licking his face, biting his hand—"playing the general tomfool," as John Thornton characterized it, the while he shook Buck back and forth and cursed him lovingly.

▶ What two desires call Buck in different directions?

For two days and nights Buck never left camp, never let Thornton out of his sight. He followed him about at his work, watched him while he ate, saw him into his blankets at night and out of them in the morning. But after two days the call in the forest began to sound more imperiously than ever. Buck's restlessness came back on him, and he was haunted by recollections of the wild brother, and of the smiling land beyond the divide and the run side by side through the wide forest stretches. Once again he took to wandering in the woods, but the wild brother came no more; and though he listened through long vigils, the mournful howl was never raised.

He began to sleep out at night, staying away from camp for days at a time; and once he crossed the divide at the head of the creek and went down into the land of timber and streams. There he wandered for a week, seeking vainly for fresh sign of the wild brother, killing his meat as he traveled and traveling with the long, easy lope that seems never to tire. He fished for salmon in a broad stream that emptied somewhere into the sea, and by this stream he killed a large black bear, blinded by the mosquitoes while likewise fishing, and raging through the forest helpless and terrible. Even so, it was a hard fight, and it aroused the last latent remnants of Buck's ferocity. And two days later, when he returned to his kill and found a dozen wolverines quarreling over the spoil, he scattered them like chaff; and those that fled left two behind who would quarrel no more.

The blood-longing became stronger than ever before. He was a killer, a thing that preyed, living on the things that lived, unaided, alone, by virtue of his own strength and prowess, surviving triumphantly in a hostile environment where only the strong survived. Because of all this he became possessed of a great pride in himself, which communicated itself like a contagion to his physical being. It advertised itself in all his movements, was apparent in the play of every muscle, spoke plainly as speech in the way he carried himself, and made his glorious furry coat if anything more glorious. But for the stray brown on his muzzle and above his eyes, and for the splash of white hair that ran midmost down his chest, he might well have been mistaken for a gigantic wolf, larger than the largest of the breed. From his St. Bernard father he had inherited size and weight, but it was his shepherd mother who had given shape to that size and weight. His muzzle was the long wolf muzzle, save that it was larger than the muzzle of any wolf; and his head, somewhat broader, was the wolf head on a massive scale.

His cunning was wolf cunning, and wild cunning; his intelligence, shepherd intelligence and St. Bernard intelligence; and all this, plus an experience gained in the fiercest of schools, made him as formidable a creature as any that roamed the wild. A carnivorous animal, living on a straight meat diet, he was in full flower, at the high tide of his life, overspilling with vigor and virility. When Thornton passed a caressing hand along his back, a snapping and crackling followed the hand, each hair discharging its pent magnetism at the contact. Every part, brain and body, nerve tissue and fiber, was keyed to the most exquisite pitch; and between all

◀ Of what is Buck proud?

◀ What traits make Buck so formidable? Which traits did he inherit and which did he learn? How did Buck learn these traits/behaviors?

the parts there was a perfect <u>equilibrium</u> or adjustment. To sights and sounds and events which required action, he responded with lightning-like rapidity. Quickly as a husky dog could leap to defend from attack or to attack, he could leap twice as quickly. He saw the movement, or heard sound, and responded in less time than another dog required to <u>compass</u> the mere seeing or hearing. He perceived and determined and responded in the same instant. In point of fact the three actions of perceiving, determining, and responding were <u>sequential</u>; but so <u>infinitesimal</u> were the intervals of time between them that they appeared simultaneous. His muscles were surcharged with vitality, and snapped into play sharply, like steel springs. Life streamed through him in splendid flood, glad and rampant, until it seemed that it would burst him asunder in sheer ecstasy and pour forth generously over the world.

"Never was there such a dog," said John Thornton one day, as the partners watched Buck marching out of camp.

"When he was made, the mold was broke," said Pete.

"Py jingo! I t'ink so mineself," Hans affirmed.

▶ How does Buck change upon entering the forest?

They saw him marching out of camp, but they did not see the instant and terrible transformation which took place as soon as he was within the secrecy of the forest. He no longer marched. At once he became a thing of the wild, stealing along softly, cat-footed, a passing shadow that appeared and disappeared among the shadows. He knew how to take advantage of every cover, to crawl on his belly like a snake, and like a snake to leap and strike. He could take a ptarmigan[5] from its nest, kill a rabbit as it

---

5. **ptarmigan.** Bird; type of grouse often hunted for food

Words For Everyday Use	e • qui • lib • ri • um (ē′kwi lib′rē um) n., state of balance	se • quen • tial (si kwen′shəl) adj., in a regular series or order
	com • pass (kum′pəs) vt., accomplish	in • fin • i • tes • i • mal (in′fin i tes′i məl) adj., too small to be measured

slept, and snap in midair the little chipmunks flee-ing a second too late for the trees. Fish, in open pools, were not too quick for him; nor were beaver, mending their dams, too wary. He killed to eat, not from wantonness; but he preferred to eat what he killed himself. So a lurking humor ran through his deeds, and it was his delight to steal upon the squir-rels, and, when he all but had them, to let them go, chattering in mortal fear to the treetops.

◄ *What "game" does Buck play with the squirrels? Why does he do this?*

As the fall of the year came on, the moose appeared in greater abundance, moving slowly down to meet the winter in the lower and less <u>rigor-ous</u> valleys. Buck had already dragged down a stray part-grown calf; but he wished strongly for larger and more formidable <u>quarry</u>, and he came upon it one day on the divide at the head of the creek. A band of twenty moose had crossed over from the land of streams and timber, and chief among them was a great bull. He was in a savage temper, and, standing over six feet from the ground, was as for-midable an antagonist as ever Buck could desire. Back and forth the bull tossed his great palmated[6] antlers, branching to fourteen points and embracing seven feet within the tips. His small eyes burned with a vicious and bitter light, while he roared with fury at sight of Buck.

From the bull's side, just forward of the flank, pro-truded a feathered arrow-end, which accounted for his savageness. Guided by that instinct which came from the old hunting days of the primordial world, Buck proceeded to cut the bull out from the herd. It was no slight task. He would bark and dance about in front of the bull, just out of reach of the great

---

6. **palmated.** Shaped like a hand, with spread fingers

Words For Everyday Use

rig • or • ous (rig´ər əs) *adj.*, very severe or harsh

quar • ry (kwôr´ē) *n.*, anything being hunted or pursued

antlers and of the terrible splay hoofs, which could have stamped his life out with a single blow. Unable to turn his back on the fanged danger and go on, the bull would be driven into paroxysms of rage. At such moments he charged Buck, who retreated craftily, luring him on by a simulated inability to escape. But when he was thus separated from his fellows, two or three of the younger bulls would charge back upon Buck and enable the wounded bull to rejoin the herd.

There is a patience of the wild—dogged, tireless, persistent as life itself—that holds motionless for endless hours the spider in its web, the snake in its coils, the panther in its ambuscade;[7] this patience belongs peculiarly to life when it hunts its living food; and it belonged to Buck as he clung to the flank of the herd, retarding its march, irritating the young bulls, worrying the cows with their half-grown calves, and driving the wounded bull mad with helpless rage. For half a day this continued. Buck multiplied himself, attacking from all sides, enveloping the herd in a whirlwind of menace, cutting out his victim as fast as it could rejoin its mates, wearing out the patience of creatures preyed upon, which is a lesser patience than that of creatures preying.

As the day wore along and the sun dropped to its bed in the northwest (the darkness had come back and the fall nights were six hours long), the young bulls retraced their steps more and more reluctantly to the aid of their beset leader. The down-coming winter was harrying them on to the lower levels, and it seemed they could never shake off this tireless creature that held them back. Besides, it was not the life of the herd,

▶ Why do the younger moose eventually leave?

---

7. **ambuscade.** Ambush

Words For Everyday Use

splay (splā) *adj.*, turning outward; spreading
par • ox • ysm (par′əks iz′əm) *n.*, sudden attack or spasm
har • ry (har′ē) *vt.*, force or push along

or of the young bulls, that was threatened. The life of only one member was demanded, which was a remoter interest than their lives, and in the end they were content to pay the toll.

As twilight fell the old bull stood with lowered head, watching his mates—the cows he had known, the calves he had fathered, the bulls he had mastered—as they <u>shambled</u> on at a rapid pace through the fading light. He could not follow, for before his nose leaped the merciless fanged terror that would not let him go. Three hundredweight more than half a ton he weighed; he had lived a long, strong life, full of fight and struggle, and at the end he faced death at the teeth of a creature whose head did not reach beyond his great knuckled knees.

From then on, night and day, Buck never left his prey, never gave it a moment's rest, never permitted it to browse the leaves of trees or the shoots of young birch and willow. Nor did he give the wounded bull opportunity to slake his burning thirst in the slender trickling streams they crossed. Often, in desperation, he burst into long stretches of flight. At such times Buck did not attempt to stay him, but loped easily at his heels, satisfied with the way the game was played, lying down when the moose stood still, attacking him fiercely when he strove to eat or drink.

The great head drooped more and more under its tree of horns, and the shambling trot grew weaker and weaker. He took to standing for long periods, with nose to the ground and dejected ears dropped limply; and Buck found more time in which to get water for himself and in which to rest. At such moments, panting with red lolling tongue and with eyes fixed upon the big bull, it appeared to Buck that

◄ How does Buck gain an advantage over his prey? What qualities does he display?

Words For Everyday Use

sham • ble (sham´bəl´) *vi.*, walk awkwardly and clumsily

a change was coming over the face of things. He could feel a new stir in the land. As the moose were coming into the land, other kinds of life were coming in. Forest and stream and air seemed <u>palpitant</u> with their presence. The news of it was borne in upon him, not by sight, or sound, or smell, but by some other and subtler sense. He heard nothing, saw nothing, yet knew that the land was somehow different; that through it strange things were afoot and ranging; and he resolved to investigate after he had finished the business in hand.

► Where does Buck head after eating his kill? Why?

At last, at the end of the fourth day, he pulled the great moose down. For a day and a night he remained by the kill, eating and sleeping, turn and turn about. Then, rested, refreshed, and strong, he turned his face toward camp and John Thornton. He broke into the long easy lope, and went on, hour after hour, never at loss for the tangled way, heading straight home through strange country with a certitude of direction that put man and his magnetic needle[8] to shame.

As he held on he became more and more conscious of the new stir in the land. There was life abroad in it different from the life which had been there throughout the summer. No longer was this fact borne in upon him in some subtle, mysterious way. The birds talked of it, the squirrels chattered about it, the very breeze whispered of it. Several times he stopped and drew in the fresh morning air in great sniffs, reading a message which made him leap on with greater speed. He was oppressed with a sense of <u>calamity</u> happening, if it were not calamity already happened; and as he crossed the last watershed and dropped down into the valley toward camp, he proceeded with greater caution.

► What does Buck sense?

---

8. **magnetic needle.** Compass for showing direction

| Words For Everyday Use | **pal • pi • tant** (pal´pə tənt) *adj.*, throbbing, quivering, trembling |
| | **ca • lam • i • ty** (kə lam ´ətē) *n.*, any extreme misfortune bringing great loss and sorrow; disaster |

Three miles away he came upon a fresh trail that sent his neck hair rippling and bristling. It led straight toward camp and John Thornton. Buck hurried on, swiftly and stealthily, every nerve straining and tense, alert to the multitudinous details which told a story— all but the end. His nose gave him a varying description of the passage of the life on the heels of which he was traveling. He remarked the pregnant silence of the forest. The bird life had flitted. The squirrels were in hiding. One only he saw—a sleek gray fellow, flattened against a gray dead limb so that he seemed a part of it, a woody excrescence upon the wood itself.

As Buck slid along with the obscureness of a gliding shadow, his nose was jerked suddenly to the side as though a positive force had gripped and pulled it. He followed the new scent into a thicket and found Nig. He was lying on his side, dead where he had dragged himself, an arrow protruding, head and feathers, from either side of his body.

◄ *What has happened to the camp?*

A hundred yards farther on, Buck came upon one of the sled-dogs Thornton had bought in Dawson. This dog was thrashing about in a death-struggle, directly on the trail, and Buck passed around him without stopping. From the camp came the faint sound of many voices, rising and falling in a singsong chant. Bellying forward to the edge of the clearing, he found Hans, lying on his face, feathered with arrows like a porcupine. At the same instant Buck peered out where the spruce-bough lodge had been and saw what made his hair leap straight up on his neck and shoulders. A gust of overpowering rage swept over him. He did not know that he growled, but he growled aloud with a terrible ferocity. For the last time in his life he allowed passion to <u>usurp</u> cunning

| Words For Everyday Use | **u • surp** (yo͞o surp) *vt.*, take over; assume power by force or without right |

and reason, and it was because of his great love for John Thornton that he lost his head.

The Yeehats were dancing about the wreckage of the spruce-bough lodge when they heard a fearful roaring and saw rushing upon them an animal the like of which they had never seen before. It was Buck, a live hurricane of fury, hurling himself upon them in a frenzy to destroy. He sprang at the foremost man (it was the chief of the Yeehats), ripping the throat wide open till the rent jugular spouted a fountain of blood. He did not pause to worry the victim, but ripped in passing, with the next bound tearing wide the throat of a second man. There was no withstanding him. He plunged about in their very midst, tearing, rending, destroying, in constant and terrific motion which defied the arrows they discharged at him. In fact, so inconceivably rapid were his movements, and so closely were the Indians tangled together, that they shot one another with the arrows; and one young hunter, hurling a spear at Buck in midair, drove it through the chest of another hunter with such force that the point broke through the skin of the back and stood out beyond. Then a panic seized the Yeehats, and they fled in terror to the woods, proclaiming as they fled the <u>advent</u> of the Evil Spirit.

And truly Buck was the Fiend <u>incarnate</u>, raging at their heels and dragging them down like deer as they raced through the trees. It was a fateful day for the Yeehats. They scattered far and wide over the country, and it was not till a week later that the last of the survivors gathered together in a lower valley and counted their losses. As for Buck, wearying of the pursuit, he returned to the desolated camp. He found Pete where he had been killed in his blankets in the

Words For Everyday Use

ad • vent (ad´ vent´) n., coming or arrival

in • car • nate (in kär´ nit) adj., endowed with a body

first moment of surprise. Thornton's desperate struggle was fresh written on the earth, and Buck scented every detail of it down to the edge of a deep pool. By the edge, head and forefeet in the water, lay Skeet, faithful to the last. The pool itself, muddy and discolored from the sluice boxes, effectually hid what it contained, and it contained John Thornton; for Buck followed his trace into the water, from which no trace led away.

All day Buck brooded by the pool or roamed restlessly about the camp. Death, as a cessation of movement, as a passing out and away from the lives of the living, he knew, and he knew John Thornton was dead. It left a great void in him, somewhat akin to hunger, but a void which ached and ached, and which food could not fill. At times, when he paused to contemplate the carcasses of the Yeehats, he forgot the pain of it; and at such times he was aware of a great pride in himself—a pride greater than any he had yet experienced. He had killed man, the noblest game of all, and he had killed in the face of the law of club and fang. He sniffed the bodies curiously. They had died so easily. It was harder to kill a husky dog than them. They were no match at all, were it not for their arrows and spears and clubs. Thenceforward he would be unafraid of them except when they bore in their hands their arrows, spears, and clubs.

Night came on, and a full moon rose high over the trees into the sky, lighting the land till it lay bathed in ghostly day. And with the coming of the night, brooding and mourning by the pool, Buck became alive to a stirring of the new life in the forest other than that which the Yeehats had made. He stood up, listening and scenting. From far away drifted a faint,

◀ *How does Buck feel about Thornton's death? What thoughts comfort him?*

◀ *What surprised Buck about killing men? How would he react to men in the future?*

Words For Everyday Use   **brood** (brō͞od) *vi.*, worry

sharp yelp, followed by a chorus of similar sharp yelps. As the moments passed the yelps grew closer and louder. Again Buck knew them as things heard in that other world which persisted in his memory.

▶ *Why is Buck ready to obey the call?*

He walked to the center of the open space and listened. It was the call, the many-noted call, sounding more luringly and compelling than ever before. And as never before, he was ready to obey. John Thornton was dead. The last tie was broken. Man and the claims of man no longer bound him.

Hunting their living meat, as the Yeehats were hunting it, on the flanks of the migrating moose, the wolf pack had at last crossed over from the land of streams and timber and invaded Buck's valley. Into the clearing where the moonlight streamed, they poured in a silvery flood; and in the center of the clearing stood Buck, motionless as a statue, waiting their coming. They were awed, so still and large he stood, and a moment's pause fell, till the boldest one leaped straight for him. Like a flash Buck struck, breaking the neck. Then he stood, without movement, as before, the stricken wolf rolling in agony behind him. Three others tried it in sharp succession; and one after the other they drew back, streaming blood from slashed throats or shoulders.

This was sufficient to fling the whole pack forward, pell-mell, crowded together, blocked and confused by its eagerness to pull down the prey. Buck's marvelous quickness and agility stood him in good stead. Pivoting on his hind legs, and snapping and gashing, he was everywhere at once, presenting a front which was apparently unbroken so swiftly did he whirl and guard from side to side. But to prevent them from getting behind him, he was forced back, down past the pool and into the creek bed, till he brought up against a high gravel bank. He worked along to a right angle in the bank which the men had made in the course of mining, and in this angle he came to bay, protected on three sides and with nothing to do but face the front.

And so well did he face it, that at the end of half an hour the wolves drew back discomfited. The tongues of all were out and lolling, the white fangs showing cruelly white in the moonlight. Some were lying down with heads raised and ears pricked forward; others stood on their feet, watching him; and still others were lapping water from the pool. One wolf, long and lean and gray, advanced cautiously, in a friendly manner, and Buck recognized the wild brother with whom he had run for a night and a day. He was whining softly, and, as Buck whined, they touched noses.

◄ Whom does Buck meet again?

Then an old wolf, gaunt and battle-scarred, came forward. Buck writhed his lips into the preliminary of a snarl, but sniffed noses with him. Whereupon the old wolf sat down, pointed nose at the moon, and broke out the long wolf howl. The others sat down and howled. And now the call came to Buck in unmistakable accents. He too sat down and howled. This over, he came out of his angle and the pack crowded around him, sniffing in half-friendly, half-savage manner. The leaders lifted the yelp[9] of the pack and sprang away into the woods. The wolves swung in behind, yelping in chorus. And Buck ran with them, side by side with the wild brother, yelping as he ran.

And here may well end the story of Buck. The years were not many when the Yeehats noted a change in the breed of timber wolves, for some were seen with splashes of brown on head and muzzle, and with a rift of white centering down the chest. But more remarkable than this, the Yeehats tell of a Ghost Dog that runs at the head of the pack. They are afraid of this Ghost Dog, for it has cunning greater than they,

◄ What changes do the Yeehats notice in the timber wolves?

---

9. **lifted the yelp.** Yelped even louder than the rest of the pack

stealing from their camps in fierce winters, robbing their traps, slaying their dogs, and defying their bravest hunters.

Nay, the tale grows worse. Hunters there are who fail to return to the camp, and hunters there have been whom their tribesmen found with throats slashed cruelly open and with wolf prints about them in the snow greater than the prints of any wolf. Each fall, when the Yeehats follow the movement of the moose, there is a certain valley which they never enter. And women there are who become sad when the word goes over the fire of how the Evil Spirit came to select that valley for an abiding-place.

In the summers there is one visitor, however, to that valley, of which the Yeehats do not know. It is a great, gloriously coated wolf, like, and yet unlike, all other wolves. He crosses alone from the smiling timberland and comes down into an open space among the trees. Here a yellow stream flows from rotted moosehide sacks and sinks into the ground, with long grasses growing through it and vegetable mold overrunning it and hiding its yellow from the sun; and here he muses for a time, howling once, long and mournfully, ere he departs.

But he is not always alone. When the long winter nights come on and the wolves follow their meat into the lower valleys, he may be seen running at the head of the pack through the pale moonlight or glimmering borealis, leaping gigantic above his fellows, his great throat a-bellow as he sings a song of the younger world, which is the song of the pack.   ∎

Responding to the Selection

Imagine that you are a young member of the Yeehat people. Discuss the myth of the Ghost Dog that you have been told by your ancestors. Describe the event that the myth explains.

Reviewing the Selection

Recalling and Interpreting

1. **R:** What does John Thornton set out to find in the East?

2. **I:** What qualities does Thornton possess that make him "unafraid of the wild"?

3. **R:** What vision comes more frequently to Buck, especially when he gazes into the fire?

4. **I:** What actions on the part of the "hairy man" in Buck's dream show his fear of the world?

5. **R:** What kind of void does John Thornton's death leave in Buck's heart?

6. **I:** What causes Buck to forget the pain of Thornton's death?

7. **R:** With whom is Buck reunited after Thornton's death?

8. **I:** What is the probable reason that Buck "sat down and howled" with the wolves?

Synthesizing

9. To what call does John Thornton, in his journey and search, respond? To what call does Buck respond?

10. Why has Buck been able to endure, survive, and master?

Understanding Literature (QUESTIONS FOR DISCUSSION)

1. Naturalism. Naturalism was a literary movement of the late nineteenth and early twentieth centuries that saw actions and events as resulting inevitably from forces in the environment. Often these forces were beyond the comprehension or control of the characters subjected to them. Identify a passage in this chapter that conveys through Buck's actions the philosophy of Naturalism. Identify the natural force that is at work. How does Buck respond to this force? Is his response effective? What point might the author be trying to make about how one should respond to overwhelming natural forces?

2. Plot and **Dénouement.** A **plot** is a series of events related to a central conflict, or struggle. A typical plot involves the introduction of a conflict, its development, and its eventual resolution. Following the resolution of a conflict is an element of plot called **dénouement.** The dénouement includes any material that ties up loose ends in the story. *The Call of the Wild* closes with a four-paragraph dénouement that begins, "And here may well end the story of Buck." What loose ends are resolved in this dénouement? What purpose is served by telling the Yeehat stories of the Ghost Dog?

Plot Analysis of *The Call of the Wild*

The following diagram, known as Freytag's Pyramid, illustrates the main parts of a plot.

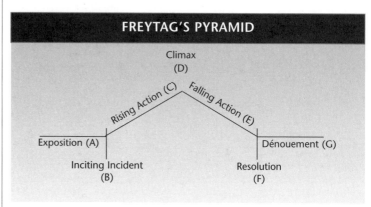

FREYTAG'S PYRAMID

Climax (D)

Rising Action (C) Falling Action (E)

Exposition (A) Dénouement (G)

Inciting Incident (B) Resolution (F)

The Parts of a Plot

A **plot** is a series of events related to a central conflict, or struggle. The **exposition** is that part of the plot that provides background information, often about the characters, setting, or conflict. The **inciting incident** is the event that introduces the central conflict. The **rising action**, or **complication**, develps the conflict to a high point of intensity. The **climax** is the high point of interest or suspense in the plot. The **falling action** is all the events that follow the climax. The **resolution** is the point at which the central conflict is ended, or resolved. The **dénouement** is any material that follows the resolution and that ties up loose ends.

Exposition (A)

Buck, a large half Saint Bernard and half Scottish shepherd dog, lives a leisurely life on a California estate. This life involves family walks, cold nights resting by a fireplace, swimming, hunting, and running around the stable yard. Buck is secure and content in his civilized life.

Inciting Incident (B)

Buck is snatched from his civilized life by Manuel, a gardener's helper. Gold has been found in the Klondike region of Canada, and people searching for gold are in need of large dogs like Buck to pull sleds. A rope is placed around Buck's neck, and for days he is held in a cage, tormented, and beaten. Buck learns a lesson about "primitive law," that a man wielding a club is always in charge. Buck is eventually taken to the North, where he sees his first snow.

Rising Action (C)

Buck finds himself in a life with no "peace, nor rest, nor a moment's safety." His job is to pull sleds across the cold, snowy Northland. To keep himself from starving, freezing, or being killed by other dogs, Buck has to rely on his wild instincts. He even fights one dog, Spitz, to the death and becomes the leader of his pack. Buck's instincts save him one day as he pulls a sled for an inept driver. Buck senses danger and refuses to go forward over the ice. He is beaten almost to death by the driver, but then he is saved by a man named John Thornton. Buck and Thornton watch the sled Buck had been pulling fall through the ice. Thornton takes Buck and nurses him back to health.

Climax (D)

Buck is deeply devoted to Thornton, protecting him whenever he can. One day Thornton makes a bet that Buck can pull a sled weighing a thousand pounds. Buck succeeds in moving the sled, and Thornton wins a great deal of money. With his winnings, Thornton decides to travel to a legendary lost gold mine. While Thornton spends long hours panning for gold, Buck spends time in the wilderness stalking animals or running with wild wolves. When he returns to camp on one occasion, he finds that everyone, including Thornton, has been killed by the Yeehats.

Falling Action (E)

Without fear, Buck attacks the Yeehats one by one. He kills several of them and drives the rest away in fear. Buck realizes that he has proved himself superior to men despite their spears, arrows, and clubs.

Resolution (F)

With Thornton gone, Buck has no attachment to civilization. As he stands in the center of the campsite he hears "the call of the wild." A pack of wolves encircle Buck. He kills one and injures others. Then one of the wolves touches his nose to Buck's, and Buck realizes that this is the wolf that he had run with earlier. Buck is accepted into the wolf pack and spends the rest of his life running with the wolves in the wild.

Dénouement (G)

After attacking the Yeehats so ferociously, Buck becomes a legend. Yeehats will never enter the area of Thornton's camp because they believe this valley to be inhabited by the Evil Spirit. Legend says that people who go to that area never return or are found slashed, surrounded by wolf prints in the snow. London adds that there is one regular visitor to the valley—"A great, gloriously coated wolf, like, and yet unlike, the other wolves." He may be seen leading a pack at night, singing the "song of the pack."

Creative Writing Activities

Creative Writing Activity A: Describing a Place

The location of most of the action of *The Call of the Wild* is important to the novel's theme. The snow, ice, and rugged conditions of the north are a constant reality for people and animals, and these conditions either make creatures stronger or destroy them. Write a descriptive piece about a place that has special meaning for you. Describe your place using vivid words and images. Your images should appeal to the reader's sense of sight, sound, smell, touch, and taste. Try to help your reader to understand the special meaning of the place and the effect that it has on you.

Creative Writing Activity B: Point of View

The Call of the Wild is unusual in that its main character is a dog. London creates in his readers strong emotions toward Buck by writing about Buck's thoughts, feelings, and experiences in a convincing way. Try your hand at writing a scene from the point of view of an animal. First, choose an animal. Then decide what will happen in your scene and what the animal's feelings will be toward the action that occurs.

Creative Writing Activity C: Creating a Character

The Call of the Wild has an interesting array of characters, all with distinct personalities. London bases his characters and their experiences on people and events from his own life. Create an interesting character of your own, based on someone from your life. First, write a physical description of your character. Then make a list of your character's most interesting personality traits. When you feel you know your character well, write a short paragraph in which you show your character doing something or interacting with others.

Creative Writing Activity D: Nature Writing

Jack London was fascinated by the rugged conditions of Yukon Territory, and he created vivid images of this area in his writing. What in nature fascinates you the most? Why does this particular aspect of nature catch your interest? Write a descriptive paragraph, a poem, or a brief dramatic scene that highlights some aspect of nature.

Critical Writing Activities

Critical Writing Activity A:
Comparing and Contrasting Two Lifestyles

Write an essay in which you compare and contrast the qualities needed to survive in a civilized and an uncivilized environment. To begin, look up in a dictionary the definitions of the word *civilized*. The word *uncivilized*, which begins with the prefix *un–*, meaning "not," is an antonym of the word *civilized*. That is, the two words are opposite in meaning. Draw a line down the middle of a clean sheet of paper. Write the word *civilized* and its definition at the top of the left-hand column; write the word *uncivilized* and its definition at the top of the right-hand column. In each column, list qualities needed to survive in that particular environment. Use these lists when you write your essay.

Critical Writing Activity B: Naturalism

Write an essay in which you define *Naturalism* and discuss what is Naturalistic about certain characters and situations of *The Call of the Wild*. To begin, be sure that you have a clear understanding of Naturalism. Refer to the Handbook of Literary Terms, page 108. Then find two or three examples of Naturalism in *The Call of the Wild*.

Critical Writing Activity C: Buck's Transformation

Discuss in an essay the transformation of Buck from a domesticated pet to a rugged animal who can survive in the wild. In your essay, answer the following questions: What is Buck's initial reaction to being kidnapped and thrust into an unfamiliar, rough environment? When does he begin to change? What causes the change? In which environment do you think Buck is happiest and most lives up to his potential? Explain your reasoning.

Critical Writing Activity D: Frontier Values

Write an essay that explains how Buck and John Thornton provide examples of frontier values such as courage, endurance, self-sufficiency, and individuality. To begin, make a list of frontier values and then find examples of behavior on the part of Buck and Thornton that exemplify each of these values.

Projects

Project A: The Search for Gold

In small groups, research and put together presentations about great gold rushes of the past. You can focus on the gold rush in the Klondike region that Jack London experienced, or you might research gold rushes that took place in other parts of North America and the rest of the world. You can also choose to focus on one small aspect of a particular gold rush, such as methods of travel, methods of searching for gold, survival techniques, or particular people and places. Try to make your presentations visually appealing by using original maps and illustrations. Be sure that each group is presenting a different topic.

Project B: An Original Board Game

In small groups, invent original board games based on Buck's journey from Judge Miller's estate to the wilderness of the north. The design of your game and the level of difficulty of your game is completely up to you and your group. Before you begin, you might want to map for yourselves the different stages of Buck's journey from civilization toward "the call of the wild." Try to use your imaginations and avoid creating straightforward question/answer trivia games.

Project C: Representing *The Call of the Wild* through Art

Choose an interesting person, animal, place, or scene in *The Call of the Wild* to represent through art. You need not feel that you are a skilled artist to complete this project. You need only to use your imagination and think about how you might represent one aspect of the novel with something other than words. You may draw or paint a picture, make a sculpture, make a collage, or construct a model, such as a model sled or a model of a camp, put together a costume based on what someone in the novel might have worn, or create a set of paper dolls. Display all the creations around the classroom.

Project D: Planning a Journey North

In the days of the gold rush in Yukon territory, many people died making their journeys north because they were not well prepared. Get into small groups and plan two trips north to pan for gold, one taking place in 1897 and one taking place in modern times. What would you have taken with you in 1897? What would you take with you now? How would you travel during each time period? How would you communicate with others? Create maps and plan what items of food, clothing, and equipment you would need for each trip. When each group is finished, you should compare notes to see which group would be best prepared for the journey.

Glossary

A

ab • ject • ly (ab´ jekt´ lē) *adv.,* miserably, wretchedly

ad • vent (ad´ vent´) *n.,* coming or arrival

a • men • i • ty (ə men´ə tē) *n.,* comfort or convenience

an • tag • o • nist (an tag´ə nist) *n.,* opponent; enemy

a • pex (ā´peks̓) *n.,* highest point

ar • du • ous (är´jo͞o əs) *adj.,* strenuous; hard

as • pire (əs pīr´) *vi.,* try, attempt; desire, aim

a • ver (ə vʉr´) *vt.,* declare to be true, affirm

B

ba • bel (bā´bəl) *n.,* confusion of voices, languages, or sounds

be • lie (bē lī´) *vt.,* disguise, misrepresent

be • set • ting (bē set´iŋ) *part.,* constantly harassing

brood (bro͞od) *vi.,* worry

C

ca • dence (kād´´ns) *n.,* rhythmic flow of sound

ca • lam • i • ty (kə lam´ə tē) *n.,* extreme misfortune bringing great loss and sorrow; disaster

cal • lous (kal´əs) *adj.,* unfeeling

cal • low • ness (kal´ō nes) *n.,* youth; immaturity; state of being inexperienced

ce • ler • i • ty (sə ler´i tē) *n.,* swiftness

com • min • gled (kəm miŋ´ gəld) *adj.,* intermixed

com • pass (kum´pəs) *vt.,* accomplish

con • cil • i • ate (kən sil´ē āt´) *vt.,* win over

con • sign • ment (kən sīn´mənt) *n.,* shipment

con • ster • na • tion (kän̓stər nā´shen) *n.,* great fear or shock

con • sul • ta • tion (kän̓səl tā´shən) *n.,* meeting to decide or plan

con • ta • gion (kən tā´ jən) *n.,* spreading of an emotion, idea, or custom from person to person until many are affected

con • va • les • cence (kän´və ləs̓əns) *n.,* gradual recovery after illness or injury

con • vey • ance (kən vā´əns) *n.,* carrying device

con • vul • sive (kən vul´ siv) *adj.,* occurring in violent fits; spasmodic

co • pi • ous (kō´pē əs) *adj.,* numerous

cov • ert (kuv´ərt) *adj.,* concealed, hidden

D

daunt (dônt) *vt.,* make afraid, intimidate

del • uge (del´ yооj) *vi.,* overwhelm as with a flood

de • mesne (di mān´) *n.,* region; domain

dis • com • fi • ture (dis kum´fi chər) *n.,* feeling of frustration and confusion

di • vers (dī´vərz) *adj.,* several

di • vine (də vīn´) *vt.,* find out by intuition

drag • gled (drag´əld) *adj.,* wet and dirty

du • bi • ous • ly (dоо´ bē əs lē) *adv.,* doubtfully, suspiciously

E

ed • dy (ed´ē) *n.,* little whirlpool

e • qui • lib • ri • um (ē´kwi lib´rē um) *n.,* state of balance

e • vince (ē vins´) *vt.,* show plainly; indicate

ex • er • tion (eg zer´shən) *n.,* effort

ex • trem • i • ty (ek strem´ə tē) *n.,* state of extreme necessity or danger

ex • ult • ant • ly (eg zult´'nt lē) *adv.,* triumphantly; rejoicingly

F

fas • ti • di • ous • ness (fas tid´ē əs nes) *n.,* oversensitiveness

floun • der (floun´dər) *vi.,* struggle awkwardly; stumble

fore • bear (fôr´ber´) *n.,* ancestor

for • mi • da • ble (fôr´mə də bəl) *adj.,* large; hard to handle

fraught (frôt) *adj.,* filled; charged; loaded

fu • tile (fyооt´'l) *adj.,* useless; vain

fu • tile • ly (fyоо´til´lē) *adv.,* ineffectively

G

ge • ni • al (jēn´yəl) *adj.,* amiable; cheerful

gin • ger • ly (jin´jər lē) *adv.,* cautiously

H

har • ry (har´ē) *vt.,* force or push along

her • ald (her´əld) *v.,* announce; introduce

he • red • i • ty (hə red´i tē) *n.,* inherited characteristics

I

ig • no • min • i • ous • ly (ig´nə min´ē əs lē) *adv.,* disgracefully; shamefully

im • par • tial (im pär´shəl) *adj.,* without prejudice or bias

im • peach • ment (im pēch´ment) *n.,* discredit

im • pend • ing (im pend´iŋ) *part.,* about to happen; threatening

im • per • i • ous • ly (im pir´ē es lē) *adv.,* with an overbearing or imperial manner

im • por • tune (im´ pôr tōōn´) *vt.,* demand, ask for urgently

in • ar • tic • u • late (in´är tik´yōō lit) *adj.,* incomprehensible, not understandable

in • car • nate (in´kär nit) *adj.,* endowed with a body

in • car • na • tion (in´kär nā´shən) *n.,* appearance in human form; embodiment of a quality or concept

in • co • her • ent (in´ kō hir'ənt) *adj.,* not logically con- nected; disjoined; rambling

in • com • pe • tence (in käm pə təns) *n.,* lack of ability or skill

in • cu • ri • ous *adj.,* (in kyoor´ē əs) uninterested

in • ex • o • ra • ble (in eks´ə rə bəl) *adj.,* that which cannot be moved or influenced; unrelenting

in • fin • i • tes • i • mal (in´fin i tes´i məl) *adj.,* too small to be measured

in • no • cu • ous • ly (in näk´yōō əs lē) *adv.,* harmlessly; dully

in • sid • i • ous (in sid´ē əs) *adj.,* sly or treacherous

in • su • lar (in´sə lər) *adj.,* detached; isolated

in • ti • mate (in´tə māt´) *vt.,* hint, imply

in • tro • spec • tive (in´trō spek´tiv) *adj.,* looking within one's own mind

ir • re • so • lute • ly (ir rez´ə lōōt´lē) *adv.,* indecisively

J

jad • ed (jād´id) *adj.,* worn out; dulled

L

lac • er • at • ed (las´ər āt´ed) *part.*, cut; wounded

la • tent (lāt´'nt) *adj.*, hidden

loath (lōth) *adj.*, hesitant, reluctant

lope (lōp) *n.*, long, easy stride

lu • gu • bri • ous • ly (lə goo´ brē əs lē) *adv.*, sadly, mournfully, often in an exaggerated manner

M

ma • li • cious (mə lish´əs) *adj.*, intentionally spiteful; harmful

ma • lig • nant (mə lig´nənt) *adj.*, wishing evil; dangerous

ma • lin • ger • er (mə liŋ´gər ər) *n.*, someone who avoids duty

man • date (man´dāt´) *n.*, command

man • i • fest • ly (man´ə fest´lē) *adv.*, clearly; obviously

ma • raud • er (mə rôd´ər) *n.*, one who raids, pillages, or plunders

met • a • mor • phose (met´ə mor´fōz´) *vt.*, change; transform

min • is • tra • tion (min´is trā´shən) *n.*, act of giving care, help, or service

mo • not • o • nous (mə nät´'n əs) *adj.*, unvarying; tiresome because unvarying

mo • rose (mə rōs´) *adj.*, gloomy; sullen

mu • ti • ny (myoot´'n ē) *n.*, revolt; rebellion against authority

N

no • mad • ic (nō mad´ik) *adj.*, wandering, moving about constantly

O

ob • du • rate (äb´ door it) *adj.*, not easily moved; stubborn

ob • lit • er • at • ed (ō blit´ər āt əd) *part.*, erased; destroyed

ob • scure • ly (əb skyoor´lē) *adv.*, unnoticed

or • dained (or dānd´) *part.*, commanded

or • tho • dox (ôr´thō däks´) *adj.*, usual; established (as in beliefs)

P

pad • dock (pad´ək) *n.*, enclosed field

pall (pôl) *n.*, covering

pal • pi • tant (pal´pə tənt) *adj.,* throbbing, quivering, trembling

pan • de • mo • ni • um (pan´də mō´nē əm) *n.,* wild noise and disorder

par • a • dox (par´ə däks´) *n.,* person, situation, or act that seems to have contradictory, unbelievable, or absurd qualities

par • ox • ysm (par´ əks iz´əm) *n.,* sudden attack or spasm

pe • cu • liar (pə kyo͞ol´yər) *adj.,* unique, strange

per • am • bu • late (pər am´byo͞o lāt´) *vi.,* walk about

per • emp • to • ri • ly (pər emp´tə rē lē) *adv.,* finally; absolutely

per • ti • nac • i • ty (pʉr´tə nās´ə tē) *n.,* stubborn persistance, obstinacy

per • vade (pər vād´) *vt.,* fill

pla • cat • ing • ly (plā´kāt´iŋ lē) *adv.,* pacifyingly; pleasingly

ple • thor • ic (plə thôr´ik) *adj.,* characterized by excess or profusion

po • tent (pōt´ ´nt) *adj.,* strong, powerful

pre • cip • i • tate (prē sip´ ə tāt´) *v.,* cause; start

pre • cip • i • tate (prē sip´ə tit) *adj.,* sudden; impetuous, rash

pre • em • i • nent • ly (prē em´ə nənt lē) *adv.,* excelling above others

pre • rog • a • tive (prē räg ` ə tiv) *n.,* right or privilege, especially one peculiar to a rank or class

pri • mor • di • al (prī môr´dē əl) *adj.,* existing from the beginning of time; primitive

prog • e • ny (präj´ə nē) *n.,* descendant; offspring

pros • trate (präs´trāt´) *adj.,* lying down

prov • o • ca • tion (präv´ə kā´shən) *n.,* something that stirs up feelings or action, especially a cause of resentment or irritation

prow • ess (prou´is) *n.,* superior ability; skill

Q

quar • ry (kwôr´ē) *n.,* anything being hunted or pursued

R

ram • pant (ram´pənt) *adj.,* flourishing

re • cess (rē′ses) *n.,* secluded place

re • cur • rent (ri kʉr′ənt) *adj.,* occurring or appearing again

re • mon • strance (ri män′ strəns) *n.,* act of complaining, protesting

rent (rent) *adj.,* torn

re • proof (ri prʊof′) *n.,* rebuke; censure

re • pug • nance (ri pug′nəns) *n.,* extreme dislike or distaste

re • sil • ien • cy (ri zil′ yens ē) *n.,* ability to bounce or spring back to shape; ability to rebound

res • o • lute • ly (rez′ə lʊot′lē) *adv.,* with determination or fixed purpose

re • solved (ri zälvd′) *adj.,* firm and fixed in purpose; determined

re • tro • gres • sion (re′trə gresh′ən) *n.,* return to a lower level or stage

rig • or • ous (rig′ər əs) *adj.,* very severe or harsh

rout (rout) *vt.,* make someone get out; force out

ruth • less (rōo̅th′lis) *adj.,* without pity

S

sa • lient (sāl′yənt) *adj.,* noticeable; prominent

sat • ed (sāt′əd) *adj.,* satisfied

se • quen • tial (si kwen′shəl) *adj.,* in a regular series or order

sham • ble (sham′bəl′) *vi.,* walk awkwardly and clumsily

shirk (shʉrk) *vt.,* neglect; evade doing something

skulk • ing (skulk′iŋ) *part.,* lurking about in a sinister way

sla • ver (slav′ər) *n.,* saliva

slov • en • ly (sluv′ən lē) *adj.,* careless; untidy; slipshod

sol • i • dar • i • ty (säl′ə dar′ə tē) *n.,* unity or agreement on an opinion or purpose

so • lil • o • quize (sə lil′ə kwīz′) *vi.,* talk to oneself

som • ber (säm′bər) *adj.,* dark, dull

spas • mod • i • cal • ly (spaz mäd′ik a lē) *adv.,* suddenly; violently; fitfully

splay (splā) *adj.,* turning outward; spreading

sub • merged (sub mʉrjd′) *adj.,* covered by water

sul • len • ly (sul′ən lē) *adv.,* showing resentment; gloomily

su • per • flu • ous (sə pʉr′flʊo əs) *adj.,* being more than is needed, excessive

sup • pres • sed • ly (sə pres´ed lē) *adv.*, with restraint

su • prem • a • cy (sə prem´ə sē) *n.*, authority

sur • charged (sʉr´chärjd´) *adj.*, overloaded; overburdened

T

tan • gi • ble (tan´jə bəl) *adj.*, touchable

terse (tʉrs) *adj.*, short; concise

tor • men • tor (tôr ment´ər) *n.*, one who causes great pain or suffering

tran • sient (tran´shənt) *adj.*, staying only for a short time

trav • ail (trə vāl´) *n.*, intense pain

U

un • couth (un kōōth´) *adj.*, uncultured; crude; strange

un • cowed (un koud´) *part.*, unafraid; unintimidated

un • du • ly (un dōō´lē) *adv.*, excessively

un • won • ted (un wän´tid) *adj.*, uncommon

u • surp (yoo sʉrp´) *vt.*, take over, assume power by force or without right

V

vaunt (vônt) *n.*, boast or brag

ve • ran • da (və ran´də) *n.*, open porch

vi • car • i • ous (vī ker´ē əs) *adj.*, experienced by imagined participation in another's experience

vig • il (vij´əl) *n.*, watch kept during normal sleeping hours

vi • ril • i • ty (və ril´ə tē) *n.*, state of having strength or vigor

vo • ra • cious (vô rā´shəs) *adj.*, greedy; ravenous

W

war • i • ly (wer´ə lē) *adv.*, cautiously

wax (waks) *vi.*, increase in strength; grow larger

wont • ed (wänt´id) *adj.*, customary; habitual; usual

wraith (rāth) *n.*, ghost or specter

wran • gle (raŋ´gəl) *vi.*, quarrel angrily and noisily

Character. A **character** is a person (or sometimes an animal) who figures in the action of a literary work. A *protagonist,* or *main character,* is the central figure in a literary work. An *antagonist* is a character who is pitted against a protagonist. *Major characters* are ones who play significant roles in a work. *Minor characters* are ones who play lesser roles. A *one-dimensional character, flat character,* or *caricature* is one who exhibits a single dominant quality, or *character trait.* A *three-dimensional, full,* or *rounded character* is one who exhibits the complexity of traits associated with actual human beings. A *static character* is one who does not change during the course of the action. A *dynamic character* is one who does change. A *stock character* is one found again and again in different literary works.

Characterization. **Characterization** is the use of literary techniques to create a character. Writers use three major techniques to create characters: direct description, portrayal of characters' behavior, and representations of characters' internal states. When using direct description, the writer, through a speaker, a narrator, or another character, simply comments on the character, telling the reader about such matters as the character's appearance, habits, dress, background, personality, motivations, and so on. When using portrayal of a character's behavior, the writer presents the actions and speech of the character, allowing the reader to draw his or her own conclusions from what the character says or does. When using representations of internal states, the writer reveals directly the character's private thoughts and emotions. See *character.*

Conflict. A **conflict** is a struggle between two forces in a literary work. A *plot* involves the introduction, development, and eventual resolution of a conflict. One side of the *central conflict* in a story or drama is usually taken by the *main character.* That character may struggle against another character, against the forces of nature, against society or social norms, against fate, or against some element within himself or herself. A struggle that takes place between a character and some outside force is called an *external conflict.* A struggle that takes place within a character is called an *internal conflict.*

Foreshadowing. **Foreshadowing** is the act of presenting materials that hint at events to occur later in a story.

Inciting Incident. See *plot.*

Mood. **Mood,** or **atmosphere,** is the emotion created in the reader by part or all of a literary work. A writer creates a mood through judicious use of concrete details.

Motivation. A **motivation** is a force that moves a character to think, feel, or behave in a certain way.

Naturalism. **Naturalism** was a literary movement of the late nineteenth and early twentieth centuries that saw actions and events as resulting inevitably from biological or natural forces or from forces in the environment. Often these forces were beyond the comprehension or control of the characters subjected to them. Taken to its extreme, Naturalism views all events as mechanically determined by external forces, including decisions made by people. Much of modern fiction, with its emphasis on social conditions leading to particular consequences is Naturalistic in this sense. Jack London was one of many authors informed by the philosophy of Naturalism.

Plot. A **plot** is a series of events related to a central *conflict*, or struggle. A typical plot involves the introduction of a conflict, its development, and its eventual resolution. Terms used to describe elements of plot include the following:

- The **exposition,** or **introduction,** sets the tone or mood, introduces the characters and the setting, and provides necessary background information.
- The **inciting incident** is the event that introduces the central conflict.
- The **rising action,** or **complication,** develops the conflict to a high point of intensity.
- The **climax** is the high point of interest or suspense in the plot.
- The **crisis,** or **turning point,** often the same event as the climax, is the point in the plot where something decisive happens to determine the future course of events and the eventual working out of the conflict.
- The **falling action** is all of the events that follow the climax.
- The **resolution** is the point at which the central conflict is ended, or resolved.
- The **dénouement** is any material that follows the resolution and that ties up loose ends.
- The **catastrophe,** in tragedy, is the event that marks the ultimate tragic fall of the central character. Often this event is the character's death.

Plots rarely contain all these elements in precisely this order. Elements of exposition may be introduced at any time in the course of a work. A work may begin with a catastrophe and then use flashback to explain it. The exposition or dénouement or even the resolution may be missing. The inciting incident may occur before the beginning of the action actually described in the work. These are but a few of the many possible variations that plots can exhibit. See *conflict*.

Protagonist. See *character*.

Setting. The **setting** of a literary work is the time and place in which it occurs, together with all the details used to create a sense of a particular time and place. Writers create setting by various means. In fiction, setting is most often revealed by means of description of such elements as landscape, scenery, buildings, furniture, clothing, the weather, and the season. It can also be revealed by how characters talk and behave. In its widest sense, setting includes the general social, political, moral, and psychological conditions in which characters find themselves.

Theme. A **theme** is a central idea in a literary work.